Cambridge Elements ≡

Elements in Quantitative and Computational Methods for the
Social Sciences
edited by
R. Michael Alvarez
California Institute of Technology
Nathaniel Beck
New York University

SURVIVAL ANALYSIS

A NEW GUIDE FOR SOCIAL SCIENTISTS

Alejandro Quiroz Flores
University of Essex

CAMBRIDGE
UNIVERSITY PRESS

CAMBRIDGE
UNIVERSITY PRESS

University Printing House, Cambridge CB2 8BS, United Kingdom

One Liberty Plaza, 20th Floor, New York, NY 10006, USA

477 Williamstown Road, Port Melbourne, VIC 3207, Australia

314–321, 3rd Floor, Plot 3, Splendor Forum, Jasola District Centre, New Delhi – 110025, India

103 Penang Road, #05–06/07, Visioncrest Commercial, Singapore 238467

Cambridge University Press is part of the University of Cambridge.

It furthers the University's mission by disseminating knowledge in the pursuit of education, learning, and research at the highest international levels of excellence.

www.cambridge.org
Information on this title: www.cambridge.org/9781009054508
DOI: 10.1017/9781009053594

© Alejandro Quiroz Flores 2022

First published 2022

A catalogue record for this publication is available from the British Library.

ISBN 978-1-009-05450-8 Paperback
ISSN 2398-4023 (online)
ISSN 2514-3794 (print)

Survival Analysis

A New Guide for Social Scientists

Elements in Quantitative and Computational Methods for the Social Sciences

DOI: 10.1017/9781009053594
First published online: May 2022

Alejandro Quiroz Flores
University of Essex

Author for correspondence: Alejandro Quiroz Flores, aquiro@essex.ac.uk

Abstract: Quantitative social scientists use survival analysis to understand the forces that determine the duration of events. This Element provides a guideline to new techniques and models in survival analysis, particularly in three areas: nonproportional covariate effects, competing risks, and multistate models. It also revisits models for repeated events. The Element promotes multistate models as a unified framework for survival analysis and highlights the role of general transition probabilities as key quantities of interest that complement traditional hazard analysis. These quantities focus on the long-term probabilities that units will occupy particular states conditional on their current state, and they are central in the design and implementation of policy interventions.

Keywords: survival analysis, event history modeling, hazard analysis, econometrics, quantitative social science, statistics

ISBNs: 9781009054508 (PB), 9781009053594 (OC)
ISSNs: 2398-4023 (online), 2514-3794 (print)

Contents

1 Introduction

Understanding the duration of events is an important part of social science research. Why are some wars longer than others? Why do convicted criminals re-offend quickly while others never re-offend? What determines the length of a spell of unemployment? Why are some democracies so durable while others revert quickly to autocracy? Understanding the forces that determine the duration of these and other events connects to some of the most essential discussions in the social sciences and contributes to the implementation and timing of public policy interventions. In order to answer questions related to duration, researchers rely on survival analysis, also known as event history modeling. Survival analysis focuses on the study of time to an event, such as the end of an interstate war if we were interested in the duration of armed conflict, or the time of a reversal to autocracy, if we were interested in the survival of democratic regimes.

This Element provides a guideline to new models, developments, and applications of survival analysis in the social sciences. Survival analysis is widely used in the social sciences, and Janet Box-Steffensmeier and Brad Jones's *Event History Modeling: A Guide for Social Scientists* (2004) has played a key role in promoting the use of these techniques. The Element assumes that readers are familiar with the concepts and applications of event history models as discussed by these authors.

Indeed, this Element covers themes that are also discussed by Box-Steffensmeier and Jones (2004), particularly nonproportional covariates, repeated events, and competing risks. However, the Element updates this material with state-of-the-art techniques developed over the past fifteen years. For instance, readers will find new guidelines for the implementation of tests for nonproportionality and refined techniques for the interpretation and visualization of time-varying covariates. On competing risks, readers will find a completely new emphasis on cumulative incidence functions, as well as different models to estimate them. Repeated events are revisited, reorganized, and updated with new techniques such as mixed models with fixed and random effects. More importantly, the Element approaches these themes from an entirely new perspective that promotes multistate models as a unified framework for survival analysis and highlights the role of transition probabilities as key quantities of interest.

In addition, readers familiar with the implementation in *Stata* of the work of Box-Steffensmeier and Jones (2004) will note that the advanced models in this Element are fully implemented in the *R Language and Environment for Statistical Computing*. This approach to software takes advantage of new models developed in biostatistics exclusively for R, thus providing researchers with an additional opportunity to update their programming skills in survival analysis.

1.1 Topics in the Element

This Element covers contributions and advances in survival analysis in the social sciences over the past fifteen years. In particular, it reviews techniques distributed over three themes: nonproportional covariates, competing risks, and multistate models. The Element also revisits models for repeated events and presents new models that generalize previous techniques. A basic understanding of these themes is necessary to take full advantage of the technical developments presented in this Element.

The Element begins with methods for the identification of nonproportional covariates in proportional models such as a Cox or a Weibull model and summarizes new techniques that facilitate the interpretation of time-varying covariates. The identification of nonproportional covariates is an essential aspect of survival analysis. However, the correct implementation of techniques that identify nonproportional covariate effects requires careful consideration of the model specification and appropriate use of timescales in the application of Grambsch and Therneau's global test (1994). This section reviews the logic of the global test and provides clear guidelines for its correct implementation. It also covers recent work on the interpretation of variables that have been turned into time-varying covariates to address a lack of proportionality. The Element relies on data on democratic breakdowns collected by Maeda (2010) to demonstrate these techniques. Maeda's data is organized in a very convenient multiple-record format, and it has been used widely in the analysis of democratic survival.

Models for repeated events have been popular in the social sciences for a number of years. These are useful models in the study of democratic transitions as countries experience repeated spells of democracy. This is also a feature of interstate conflict, as country dyads experience repeated spells of war. Repeated events models are also applied to other topics, such as unemployment or incarceration. As popular as the models of repeated events are, the terminology used in the literature is often confusing. Moreover, technical aspects of the correct duration setup for these models also generate some confusion, such as the use of elapsed-time or gap-time as dependent variables, or the role of stratification. This section on repeated events aims at bringing more clarity to these models, their format, and their comparative advantages. Moreover, the section reviews recent additions to the menu of models, including the conditional frailty model that combines a frailty parameter with the ability to stratify hazard rates, as well as mixed models with fixed and random effects as more general cases of frailty models. The section also relies on Maeda's data (2010) to revisit models of repeated events. Maeda's data is a good candidate for this type of analysis, as it covers multiple countries with multiple spells of democracy.

The Element covers alternative approaches to competing risks models, and it assumes familiarity with basic competing risks analysis in order to interpret them as special cases of more general multistate models. In this light, the section shifts the focus from the analysis of hazard rates to the study of cumulative incidence functions and more general transition probabilities. In doing so, the section points at the incorrect use of naïve survivor functions and the correct computation of quantities of interest. In order to analyze the effect of covariates on incidence functions, the section presents Fine and Gray's (1999) model and its practical implementation. Again, this section uses Maeda's data (2010) to demonstrate the application of new techniques in the analysis of competing risks. In fact, Maeda's original goal was to explore competing risks present in democratic breakdowns, and therefore, it provides an excellent source of information.

Lastly, the Element presents essential concepts and definitions for multistate models. These models have been available in biostatistics for more than twenty years, but researchers have only just begun to apply them to substantive questions in the social sciences. Multistate models are the most general type of survival models, and they nest many techniques that have been widely used in the social sciences. Multistate models can be complex and require a good understanding of probability and Markov models. In this light, the section introduces the key structure and probability aspects of multistate models and reviews the importance of nonparametric estimators such as the Nelson–Aalen estimator of the cumulative hazard rate and the Aalen–Johansen estimator of the matrix of transition probabilities.

The section presents an application of an illness-death multistate model to the implementation of nonpharmaceutical interventions (NPIs) in US universities during the Covid-19 pandemic. The application works out in detail the necessary steps in preparing data for the estimation of multistate models, provides a step-by-step guide to the calculation of transition probabilities, and connects them to the Aalen–Johansen estimator of the matrix of transition probabilities using a Cox proportional hazards model. The section relies on very recent data collected by Cevasco et al. (2020) for more than 570 universities in the USA and the specific time of their NPIs during the pandemic, thus making it an ideal candidate to study multistate models. The subject is also important in the context of the Covid-19 pandemic and shows the importance of this type of analysis in the implementation of policy interventions.

1.2 A Different Approach to Survival Analysis

The Element highlights the role of cumulative incidence functions and transition probabilities in survival analysis. These quantities are central to multistate models and focus on the long-term probabilities that units will occupy a state at some time t given that they occupy a different state at some other time v. This approach allows researchers to answer questions such as what is the probability that a country that has been democratic for ten years will be autocratic next year? Or what is the probability that an individual will be in employment in six months given that they are currently unemployed? Or what is the probability that an interstate crisis will escalate into a full-scale war in three weeks, and what is the probability that this war will come to a conclusion six months after it first started? Indeed, transition probabilities allow researchers to answer very complex questions, and this Element promotes the use of these quantities in social science applications of survival models.

This approach complements the analysis of hazard rates popular in the social sciences, and the Element assumes that researchers will begin their empirical analysis with an exploration of hazard functions and the effect of covariates on this essential quantity. This is why the first section provides new guidelines for the identification of nonproportional covariates and their interpretation in the context of hazard rate analysis. Moreover, the computation of transition probabilities in multistate models is based on hazard rates via basic relationships between different probability functions. In this sense, hazard rates are crucial in more advanced models as they provide the building blocks for computation.

However, researchers must choose carefully the quantities of interest that best answer duration-related questions. The analysis of hazards rates focuses on the forces that determine transitions between states. In this light, hazard rates help us understand why covariates may increase or decrease the rates at which units experience an event over time. In the application to the implementation of nonpharmaceutical interventions across US universities presented in Section 5, an analysis of hazard rates will help us understand, for example, whether the number of students in a university determines the rate at which an institution implements a policy of online teaching and remote work. However, from a perspective of transition probabilities, the focus is, for example, on the probability that a university that has not implemented any intervention by March 15, 2020, will be closing its campus on March 19. This type of question is particularly relevant in the implementation of interventions, and this is why these quantities of interest have been central in biostatistics, as clinicians must make decisions about the future state of patients given their current condition. In other words, rather than estimating whether a covariate changes the hazard rate for a particular transition, the focus in multistate models is on estimating the probabilities that units will be in different states at different points in time. This is the essence of transition probabilities.

The Element demonstrates these techniques using the *R Language and Environment for Statistical Computing*. The application of survival models in the social sciences has relied mostly on *Stata*, as it provides easy-to-use models as well as excellent coverage of fully parametric models, such as the Weibull or the log-normal models. However, advances in survival analysis have taken place mostly in biostatistics, which now relies heavily on *R*.

At the time of writing, *R* provides the most up-to-date suite of advanced models and processes, including packages that facilitate the interpretation of time-varying covariates, the estimation of conditional frailty and mixed models for repeated events, and the computation of cumulative incidence functions in competing risks, among other advanced features. More prominently, there are multiple *R* packages to prepare data for the analysis of multistate models, which is, without doubt, the most complex part of the estimation of these models. These packages also provide enormous flexibility for the estimation of a wide menu of multistate models and the interpretation of the very complex effects of covariates on transition probabilities. For these reasons, the Element relies on the *R* language for the demonstration of the aforementioned techniques. Readers can click on the following link for analysis and replication code in the author's Dataverse repository: https://doi.org/10.7910/DVN/ADZUEA.

1.3 Choosing Models

This Element approaches the modeling of duration processes from a multistate perspective. Quantitative social scientists have recently begun to estimate multistate survival models (e.g. Metzger & Jones, 2016), which have been used in biostatistics for almost twenty years. Multistate models are very useful generalizations of traditional techniques such as models for single events used in analyses of political survival, competing risks for types of autocratic reversals, repeated events for state policy adoption, and even bivariate models, which are special cases of multistate models. Section 5 presents multistate models in detail, but at this point, it is convenient to introduce them briefly as a framework for model selection.

Consider a stochastic process X_t that denotes the state occupied by a unit at time t. For instance, a country at time t may occupy one of two states: democracy (state 1) or autocracy (state 3). Specifically, a country may be democratic at time v, with $X_v = 1$, and autocratic at time $t > v$, with $X_t = 3$. However, it is perfectly possible that a country may transition again from autocracy at time t to democracy at time u, where $u > t > v$. Note that the numbers that denote states are just labels that differentiate these states and they do not necessarily indicate an order or sequence. In some cases, however, there may be a temporal sequence of events, and therefore, it is recommended that the labels of states reflect the order of the sequence, if such sequence exists.

Multistate models have two large classes of states: transitioning states, which can be visited multiple times (units may enter and exit those states), and absorbing states, which can be visited only one time (units may only enter those states but cannot exit them). Death is a very good example of an absorbing state, while remission from a chronic condition is often a transitioning state. Absorbing states in social sciences may be more difficult to find. Instead, many states of substantive interest tend to be transitioning. The alternating states of democracy and autocracy are excellent examples.

Multistate models must also define whether there is an initial state. Initial states are convenient for analytical purposes and may capture realistic initial conditions. In a typical biostatistics example, the initial state for individuals may be the state "alive" while the next state in the process is "death," which is an absorbing state. Initial states are also difficult to find in the social sciences, partly because we may not know the historical conditions for a particular process. Yet multistate models may be estimated in the absence of initial conditions and units may enter the analysis from multiple states. For instance, in the analysis of institutional change and democratization, there is no initial state, and technically, any country can transition from a democracy to an autocracy, and vice versa. In this context, the state democracy (state 1) and the state autocracy (state 3) may be transitioning states.

The previous discussion indicates that multistate models also allow for more than two states. In the institutional change example, countries may backslide from democracy (state 1) to a mixed regime (state 2) to a full autocracy (state 3). For instance, using the ratings of the Freedom House Index, Tanzania was a free regime from 2000 to 2004, a partly free regime in 2005, a not free regime in 2006, a partly free regime from 2007 to 2013, and a not free regime from 2014.[1] Moreover, multistate models also allow for multiple absorbing and transitioning states. As argued previously, it is perfectly possible to assume that autocracy and democracy are transitioning states, as there is no guarantee that a country will stay autocratic or democratic forever.

These discussions point to the importance of data organization in survival analysis and the correct coding of right- and left-censored units. As long as units are correctly coded and the software of choice for empirical analysis correctly

---

[1] https://freedomhouse.org

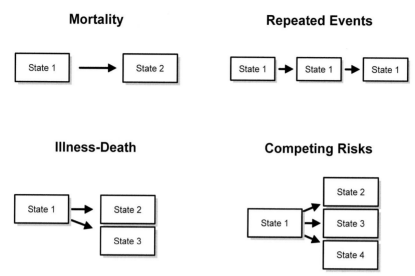

Figure 1 Examples of survival models. Each arrow represents a potential transition. Adapted by permission from Springer Nature Customer Service Centre GmbH: Springer Nature, Analysis of Multivariate Survival Data by Hougaard, 2000

captures entry and exit times, as well as failures, particularly for multiple-record data, estimation is straightforward. However, the data setup of some multistate models is slightly more complex, and the format of the data, and even the labels of variables and covariates, must be adjusted for available packages. Fortunately, there are *R* packages such as *mstate* that help set the data correctly (Putter, Fiocco, & Geskus, 2007) with estimation remaining relatively simple. Figure 1 presents a diagram of several survival models, including some multistate models such as the illness-death model.

Starting from the top-left of Figure 1 and moving clockwise, the first model is a typical mortality model where all units have the same initial state and can only transition to a single absorbing state. Traditional survival models of war or models of leader tenure are good examples of mortality models whereby all units share an initial state and may transition to one absorbing state – peace in the case of war or deposition in the case of leader tenure. The second model represents a structure of repeated events that is suitable for the analysis of multiple democratic spells (e.g. Maeda, 2010) and that can be extended to models of alternating states, as demonstrated by Metzger and Jones (2016).

In the competing risks model presented at the bottom right of Figure 1, all units share the same initial state, and they can transition to multiple states, all of them absorbing. Competing risks models are widely used in the social sciences, including applications to types of leader depositions, the types of transitions from democracy, or the analysis of CEO turnover. The Element makes extensive use of Maeda's data and analysis of two modes of democratic breakdowns: those where an external force topples a democratic government and those where a democratic leader suspends the democratic process.

Competing risks models provide an excellent opportunity to introduce more complex multistate models, which can be derived from repeated experiments of competing risks structures (Beyersmann, Allignol, & Schumacher, 2012). The last model in Figure 1 is known as an illness-death model or as a disability model. This model is used in Section 5 to analyze the NPIs of US universities during the Covid-19 pandemic. The model explores transitions from an initial state where no interventions were implemented to a state where remote working was in place. Universities also closed their campuses in response to the crisis, and the multistate analysis of Section 5 models transitions from the initial state to remote working to campus closures but also transitions from the initial condition to campus closure. There are many versions of the illness-death model; the version used in Figure 1 and Section 5 is a model without recovery.

Approaching survival analysis from a multistate perspective improves our ability to model complex processes. In some cases, the selection of a modeling framework is straightforward, particularly if the data can only support a particular model. For instance, if a study only records the tenure of heads of government and not how they lose office, the only available option for analysis is a traditional mortality model. However, if the study records multiple spells in office, this can be transformed into a model of alternating states or a model of repeated events. However, it is unlikely that this data will allow for a competing risks model.

Having selected a modeling framework researchers also need to decide which model to use to estimate the effect of covariates. Often, researchers make a choice from fully parametric models such as Weibull model and semi-parametric models such as Cox or between different types of fully parametric models, for instance, Weibull as opposed to log-normal. While there are important trade-offs between these modeling techniques, the Element focuses on the estimation of the Cox proportional hazards model.

1.4 Notation

Consider a continuous, positive random variable T that indicates time to an event.[2] The potential realizations t of T are determined by a probability distribution. For instance, countries experience sequences of democratic and autocratic

---

[2] This Element focuses on time T as a continuous random variable, but there is also new applied work on T as a discrete variable (e.g. Boehmke, 2009; Carter & Signorino, 2010).

spells, and t may be the number of years, or even days, that a country is considered to be democratic before it backslides to autocracy.

Define the probability density function of T as follows:

$$f(t) = \lim_{\Delta t \to 0} \frac{Pr(t \leq T \leq t + \Delta t)}{\Delta t}. \tag{1}$$

This is the probability that the event of interest, such as a transition to autocracy, will take place in the small interval of time t and $t + \Delta t$ as Δt goes to zero.

The cumulative density function is given by:

$$F(t) = Pr(T \leq t) = \int_0^t f(u)du. \tag{2}$$

This is the probability that the event of interest will take place before and including time t. In the example of democratic backsliding, and measuring time in days, $F(365)$ is the probability that democracy will transition to autocracy in 365 or fewer days. The complement of $F(t)$, known in survival analysis as the survivor function $S(t)$, is given by $S(t) = Pr(T > t) = 1 - Pr(T \leq t)$. In the example of democratic transitions, this is the probability that democracy will remain – or survive – as democracy for more than 365 days.

The hazard rate $\lambda(t)$ plays a key role in survival analysis. The hazard rate is a conditional rate given by:

$$\lambda(t) = \lim_{\Delta t \to 0} \frac{Pr(t \leq T \leq t + \Delta t | T \geq t)}{\Delta t} = \frac{f(t)}{S(t)}. \tag{3}$$

This is the rate at which units experience the event of interest in the small interval t and $t + \Delta t$ as Δt goes to zero given that they have not experienced the event at the beginning of that interval. In the previous example, this is the rate at which democracies backslide, say, in between days 365 and 366 given that that they are democratic at the very beginning of day 365.[3] The hazard rate is the ratio of the probability density function to the survivor function such that $\lambda(t) = f(t)/S(t)$.

In order to compute key quantities of interest in multistate models, researchers should also be familiar with the integrated hazard. Integrated hazards provide important information about the hazard rate, such as the speed at which risk is accumulated over time. The integrated hazard, also known as the cumulative hazard, is given by:

$$\Lambda(t) = \int_0^t \lambda(u)du. \tag{4}$$

---

[3] Some texts will refer to the hazard rate as the instantaneous probability that a unit will experience the event of interest in the small interval t and $t + \Delta t$, and it is not unusual to find the hazard rate denoted as $\lambda(t)dt$, where dt is the infinitesimal interval $[t, t + dt]$ (e.g. Borgan, 1997; Beyersmann, Allignol, & Schumacher, 2012).

The cumulative hazard is crucial for computing other quantities of interest. In Sections 4 and 5, the following version of the survivor function as determined by the cumulative hazard will be particularly useful:

$$S(t) = \exp(-\Lambda(t)). \tag{5}$$

Lastly, researchers should consider the following reinterpretation of the CDF. This is important for the construction of cumulative incidence functions, which play a key role in the analysis of competing risks. Since $f(t) = \lambda(t)S(t)$ and $F(t) = \int_0^t f(u)du$, then $F(t)$ can be rewritten as follows:

$$F(t) = \int_0^t \lambda(u)S(u)du. \tag{6}$$

Rewriting $F(t)$ in this way is mathematically convenient but also substantively interesting. As an example, consider a unit in an initial state m at time v with the potential of experiencing an event l at some future time t such that $l \neq m$. This could be a democratic country with the potential to experience a transition to autocracy. This reformulation of $F(t)$ explores the probability that the event of interest – the transition from m to l – will take place before and including time t as a function of two forces in tension with each other. The hazard rate $\lambda(t)$ is a transition force that pulls the unit away from state m toward state l. However, the survivor function, by definition, keeps the unit in state m. As it will be explained in Section 5, understanding $F(t)$ as the result of forces pulling in opposite directions will be essential in modeling multistate processes, including competing risks.

1.5 Summary

This Element promotes multistate models as a unified framework for survival analysis. Survival models are often introduced to students in a modular form that often begins with a mortality model. However, the survival models used in the social sciences may also be approached as special cases of more general multistate models. From a multistate perspective, units occupy a state for a period of time, and some of them experience a transition to another state. From this perspective, it is possible to analyze the spells of time spent in particular states, as well as the probabilities of occupying a particular state at different points in time, which naturally entails an analysis of the likelihood of transitions between states. This logic is very flexible and can be extended to more complex situations where units may transition to competing states, where some of those states can be experienced multiple times, and where units may enter and exit different states multiple times. This is the logic of multistate models.

1.6 Further Readings

The Element assumes that readers are familiar with Janet Box-Steffensmeier and Brad Jones's *Event History Modeling: A Guide for Social Scientists* (2004). Readers are encouraged to study two key books that have shaped survival analysis in biostatistics: Hougaard's *Analysis of Multivariate Survival* (2000) and Therneau and Grambsch's *Modeling Survival Data: Extending the Cox Model* (2000). These books provide essential coverage of the topics in this Element, and modern *R* packages can now implement many of the complex models covered by these authors. The package *survival*, written by Therneau et al. (2021), is central to the estimation of survival models in *R*.

2 Nonproportional Covariates

Consider the mortality model where all units share the same initial state and may transition to a single absorbing state. The mortality model is used widely because it is intuitive and provides traction to address significant challenges in applied settings, such as time-varying covariates, right- and left-censoring, fully parametric and semi-parametric methods, standard errors robust to lack of independence, tests for nonproportionality, as well as useful simulation methods. Due to its simplicity and reach, the mortality model provides an excellent opportunity to discuss important advances in event history modeling. Specifically, this section presents new guidelines to identify nonproportional covariate effects and techniques to interpret time-varying covariates.

The guidelines presented in this Element are demonstrated with the Cox proportional hazard model, which is the most popular model in the analysis of duration processes. The appeal of the Cox model is mostly derived from its simplicity, which is directly connected to the assumption of proportional covariate effects. Indeed, the proportionality assumption is essential because it simplifies estimation and facilitates the calculation of the probability density and survivor functions. While there are alternative specifications of the hazard rate, including options that do not require proportional covariates, they come with increased estimation and computational complexity and may only be applicable to specific forms of the baseline hazard. In contrast, the Cox model is applicable to any arbitrary baseline hazard and facilitates the analysis of the effect of covariates. Other popular models such as the Weibull or the exponential models also rely on the proportionality assumption and therefore share with the Cox model its flexibility and wide applicability.

Nevertheless, the trade-off between simplicity and proportionality in the Cox model is important: when covariate effects are not proportional, the power of the tests for these nonproportional variables decreases, and their effects over time may be overestimated (Schemper, 1992). Since the Cox model focuses on the effects of covariates on the hazard rate, breaking the proportionality assumption simply obliterates the raison d'être of the Cox model.

The Cox models estimated throughout the Element use the Efron method for ties. This method is more accurate for data with large numbers of ties, and it is not computationally intensive. The number of ties in the Maeda data set (2010) is not large, and therefore, estimation results using the Efron and the Exact methods are the same up to the first decimal point. However, it must be noted that the Exact method for ties is not available for the mixed-effects Cox model and for Fine and Gray's model of competing risks. The Exact method for ties in multistate models, while technically possible, is numerically intensive and excessively long for the purposes of this Element.

This section revisits the concept of proportional covariates in the context of democratic breakdowns. It elaborates on the logic behind Grambsch and Therneau's test for nonproportionality, discusses challenges that obscure the interpretation of tests, and presents methods that facilitate the interpretation of time-varying covariates as the result of corrections to nonproportionality.

2.1 An Initial Application to Democratic Durability

This Element relies on Maeda's data on democratic durability (2010) to demonstrate new techniques in survival analysis. Maeda explores models of democratic durability with a focus on types of democratic termination. He argues that a democratic government may be terminated by forces outside government – such as a coup – and by democratic leaders that end the democratic process itself – such as suspending a constitution. These two types of terminations, labeled exogenous and endogenous, respectively, are explored from two different perspectives. First, Maeda estimates a traditional mortality model where the event of interest is democratic termination. Second, Maeda proceeds to estimate models of competing risks of types of democratic terminations.

Maeda (2010) explains clearly his definition of democracy and how duration is measured, as well as the covariates that determine the survival process, including level of economic development, economic growth, institutional structures, type of government, ethnic fractionalization, and urbanization, among other variables. Maeda's analysis tackles a long-standing question in political science, and his data set is ideal for survival analysis.

The unit of analysis in Maeda's (2010) data is the country-democratic spell-month, and it is organized as multiple-record data. In other words, the unit of analysis is a country's democratic spells measured at the monthly level. For instance, Argentina has two different democratic spells. The first democratic

Table 1 An example of a democratic spell: Argentina 1973–1976. Data from Maeda (2010).

Country ID	Country	Year	Month	Spell ID	End	Type End	Duration
160	Arg	1973	3	2	0	0	1
160	Arg	1973	4	2	0	0	2
160	Arg	1973	5	2	0	0	3
.	.	.	.	.	.	.	.
.	.	.	.	.	.	.	.
.	.	.	.	.	.	.	.
160	Arg	1976	1	2	0	0	35
160	Arg	1976	2	2	0	0	36
160	Arg	1976	3	2	1	1	37

spell is recorded from March 1973 to March 1976, when it ends in autocratic reversal. The second spell is recorded from October 1976, and it is right-censored on December 2004. Table 1 presents a snapshot of the data.

The dependent variable in Maeda's analysis is the number of months of a democratic spell. This is shown in the column *Duration* in Table 1. The median duration is 193 months, with a maximum duration of 2,350 months. Long durations are recorded for countries with well-established democracies such as those in the USA, Canada, or the UK. Altogether, there are 108 countries in the data set and 141 democratic spells. Seventy-two countries do not experience repeated spells of democracy, while 28 countries have 2 spells, 7 countries have 3 spells, and 1 country, Turkey, has 4 spells of democracy. Interestingly, there are only 45 breakdowns of democracy; this is a significant number in the context of 141 democratic spells. However, in the multiple-record data originally used by Maeda, this means that there are only 45 failures in a data set with more than 28,000 observations. The data do not include spells for periods of autocracy.

Table 2 presents a Cox proportional hazards model of democratic breakdowns. This is the traditional mortality model shown in Figure 1. Estimation was implemented using the package *survival* in *R*, and the results are identical to Maeda's results up to three decimal points. Having said this, recall that the hazard rate of a Cox model is given by:

$$\lambda(t) = \lambda_0(t)\exp(Z\beta), \tag{7}$$

where Z is an $n \times J$ matrix of j covariates where $j = 1,\ldots,J$ is the number of covariates and n is the number of observations. Note that the Cox model

Table 2 Cox proportional hazards model of democratic breakdowns. Unit: Democratic spell-month. Standard errors in parentheses clustered at the country level. Estimation results produced by the following *R* code: cox1<-coxph(Surv(t0,t,d, type="counting", origin=0) ~ Zs, data=maeda, ties="efron", id=demid, cluster=country, robust=T, x=T). Note that Surv() uses a (start,stop) counting format with a numerical censoring indicator d

Variable	Coefficient
Development	−0.7 (0.3)
Growth	−0.1 (0.0)
Presidential System	0.6 (0.7)
Mixed System	0.4 (0.9)
Majority Government	−0.6 (0.3)
Ethnic Fragmentation	−0.9 (0.8)
Trade Openness	−0.0 (0.0)
Urbanization	−0.0 (0.0)
Post–Cold War Era	−0.1 (0.4)
Imposed Policy	−0.1 (0.4)
Colony	0.1 (0.7)
Military	−0.1 (0.4)
Regional Democracy Level	−0.1 (0.1)
Observations	28, 468
Failures	42

does not include a constant term. The baseline hazard rate $\lambda_0(t)$ remains unparametrized. The focus of the Cox model is the effect of covariates on the hazard rate.

The *survival* package in *R* produces coefficients, exponentiated coefficients, and two sets of standard errors, one for a naïve variance-covariance matrix that assumes that observations are independent and one for a variance-covariance matrix that clusters the errors by country. Researchers may focus on the sign of coefficients – positive coefficients indicate an increase in the hazard rate – and whether they are statistically different from zero. Alternatively, exponentiated coefficients represent hazard ratios, and therefore, researchers should test if they are statistically different from one. Jones and Metzger (2019) provide further guidance on how to interpret estimation results from Cox models. In this particular example, the coefficient for *Development*, measured as GDP per capita, is negative and different from zero at the 95 percent confidence level. In this light, an increase in GDP per capita decreases the hazard rate of a democratic breakdown.

2.2 Proportionality in Models of Democratic Breakdowns

The Cox model is a proportional hazards model, which means that *covariates are assumed to have a proportional effect on the hazard rate over time*. Recall that the hazard rate of a Cox model is given by $\lambda(t) = \lambda_0(t) \exp(Z\beta)$. The baseline hazard $\lambda_0(t)$ may be interpreted as the "natural" rate of experiencing the event of interest over time. The baseline hazard can also be interpreted as the rate when all covariates are set to zero, although it is important to recall that a Cox proportional hazards model does not have an intercept.

Human beings, for instance, may have a high hazard rate of death at an early age, which then drops over time only to increase again as we age. When the effects of covariates are proportional, they shift the baseline hazard up and down in the same scale over time, which means that the shape of the hazard over time remains relatively unchanged. In other words, if covariate effects are proportional, changes to the hazard rate should be proportional to the baseline hazard, and that proportion should remain relatively constant over time. For instance, smoking causes harm, and the assumption is that smoking will shift the entire hazard rate for smokers above the baseline: smokers experience death at a higher rate than the baseline nonsmoker. However, the shape of the hazard rates of a smoker and a nonsmoker should be similar over time, and the only difference is that the entire hazard for a smoker is higher.

Proportionality is also explained in terms of the hazards of two individuals or units. For instance, consider a democracy's risk of autocratic reversal. Research indicates that all else equal, wealthy democracies are less likely to transition to autocracy than poorer democracies (e.g. Przeworski et al., 2000). If this is correct and if wealth had a proportional effect on the hazard rate of democracy, then poor democracies should have higher hazard rates than wealthy democracies, and the difference between the hazard rates of these two types of countries should be constant over the entire duration of the democratic spell.

To further illustrate this concept, consider two democratic countries with wide differences in terms of wealth: Nepal and Japan. In 2019, Nepal had a GDP per capita of $859 constant 2010 US dollars, while Japan had a GDP per capita of $49,187.8 in the same year. If β is the effect of GDP per capita on the hazard rate of democracies, then the hazard rate of Nepal is $\lambda_{Nepal}(t) = \lambda_0(t) \exp(\$859\beta)$, and the hazard rate of Japan is

$\lambda_{Japan}(t) = \lambda_0(t)\exp(\$49187\beta)$. In this case, the ratio of the hazard rates of Japan relative to Nepal is as follows:

$$\frac{\lambda_{\text{Japan}}(t)}{\lambda_{\text{Nepal}}(t)} = \frac{\lambda_0(t)\exp(\$49187\beta)}{\lambda_0(t)\exp(\$859\beta)} = \exp((\$49187-\$859)\beta) = \exp(\$48328\beta).$$

$$(8)$$

In terms of proportionality, the key is that this ratio is not a function of time. When the ratio is a function of time, proportionality is lost and with it the practicality of the Cox model, which is now providing incorrect results. As mentioned before, proportional covariates are necessary for the estimation of the Cox model, and without them, the model cannot be correctly implemented.

2.3 Grambsch and Therneau's Global Test of Nonproportionality

This section focuses on the global test of nonproportionality developed by Grambsch and Therneau (1994), which is the most widely used test in the social sciences. Given the importance of the test, the section provides a brief overview of the intuition behind this test. This will also bring clarity to how the test should be implemented in order to avoid errors.

First, suppose that the effect of a covariate Z on a survival process T can be estimated with a Cox model with hazard rate $\lambda(t) = \lambda_0(t)\exp(Z\beta)$. Now suppose that the process T can be partitioned in t stages and that for each stage t, it is possible to estimate a separate Cox model, each with an estimate of β_t. This would yield t-estimates of β_t of a covariate Z on the hazard rate. If the effect of the covariate Z is proportional over the hazard rate of the entire process, then we would expect that $\beta_t \forall t$ should be very similar to β. In other words, the estimate of β for a proportional covariate should be independent of time, and intuitively, a regression of all β_ts on duration should show that duration is not statistically significant. This is why an older version of the test recommended the estimation of multiple Cox models at different stages of duration time and exploring if the estimated coefficients differed significantly (Box-Steffensmeier & Jones, 2004).

The previous logic provides a good introduction to the test developed by Grambsch and Therneau (1994). For simplicity, consider again a Cox model with hazard rate $\lambda(t) = \lambda_0(t)\exp(Z\beta)$ and only one covariate Z; the authors present a model for j covariates with $j = 1, 2, \ldots, J$, but the section focuses on $j = 1$. A model of time-varying coefficients implies the following:

$$\beta(t) = \beta + g(t)\theta, \qquad (9)$$

where $g(t)$ is a function of time, and it may have a mean of zero; $g(t)$ must be a predictable process. The time-varying coefficients model is a proportional model if $\beta(t) = \beta$, which is true when $\theta = 0$. Grambsch and Therneau (1994: 516) find that "the score test for $H_0 : \beta(t) = \beta$ is equivalent to a generalized least squares test on the Schoenfeld residuals." Schoenfeld residuals are defined as $r_k(\beta) = Z_k - M(\beta, t_k)$, where Z_k is the covariate of a unit experiencing the event at time t_k and $M(\beta, t_k)$ is the conditional weighted mean of the covariate at time t_k, where $k = 1, 2, \ldots, d$ is an index of event times. A detailed definition of the term $M(\beta, t_k)$ is beyond the scope of this Element, but it represents the covariate weighted by the section of the hazard rate that involves $\exp(Z\beta)$ after estimation of the Cox partial likelihood.

Grambsch and Therneau show that the conditional expected value of the Schoenfeld residuals $E(r_k(\beta)|F_{t_k}) \simeq V(\beta, t_k)g(t_k)\theta$, where $V(\beta, t_k)$ is the conditional variance of the covariate at time t_k and F_{t_k} is a right-continuous filtration. A filtration is an ordered σ-algebra that can be interpreted as a subset of the event space; in this case, it is indexed by time and specifies the history of the process. The symbol $\simeq$ represents equipollence. More importantly, they show that the expected value of the scaled Schoenfeld residuals $r_k^* = V^{-1}(\beta, t_k)r_k(\beta)$ is $E(r_k^*|F_{t_k}) \simeq g(t_k)\theta$.

The key to the test is that it is possible to estimate a linear model of r_k^* on a function $g(t_k)$ of time, with a chi-square test for $\theta = 0$. In other words, under the null hypothesis of proportional covariates, a regression of scaled Schoenfeld residuals on a function of time should yield $\hat{\theta} = 0$. This is why in applied settings we look for high p-values in the Grambsch and Therneau global test. Grambsch and Therneau (1994: 516) refers to this procedure as a "regression approach to tests for nonproportionality."

2.3.1 Model Specification

In quantitative analysis, researchers should address potential mis-specification, particularly if they are interested in modeling the distribution of an outcome variable. Mis-specification is generally a problem because it is almost impossible to know with certainty the true specification of a model, both in terms of the selection of covariates and their functional form. In this case, theory and expertise are useful guides in specifying a model.

In the context of survival analysis, Keele (2010) finds that mis-specification has negative consequences for the identification of nonproportional covariates. Specifically, Keele finds that Grambsch and Therneau's global test may be detecting a mis-specification problem rather than nonproportional covariates. In other words, if there is mis-specification, the test may produce a false positive result. This is very problematic because in correcting a false nonproportional covariate by interacting it with a function of duration, a researcher might be estimating a model with true nonproportional covariates. In other words, in fixing a problem that is not actually there, researchers may be creating a real problem that will lead to incorrect results.

In order to avoid this, Keele (2010) argues that the correct functional form of covariates may be found using polynomials or splines of the covariates. Researchers also need to be aware that Grambsch and Therneau's test also assumes heteroscedasticity (Metzger & Jones, 2021). Subject area expertise may also inform model specification. Having done this, researchers may implement Grambsch and Therneau's global test with more confidence. However, researchers also need to exercise caution and consider the potential overfitting that may arise from an excessive use of polynomials or splines. Again, in trying to find a specification that minimizes the likelihood of a false-positive test for nonproportional covariates, researchers may estimate a model that has poor performance in test data. Unfortunately, an exploration of performance of survival models is beyond the scope of this Element.

2.3.2 Functions of Time

Often, researchers estimate a survival model and immediately run post-estimation tests, including Grambsch and Therneau's global test. As previously mentioned, the test relies on a model of the scaled Schoenfeld residuals r_k^* on a function $g(t_k)$ of time. Grambsch and Therneau do argue that different specifications for $g(t_k)$ will result in different tests. Consequently, it is important that researchers consider the options for $g(t_k)$ carefully and apply them correctly. Grambsch and Therneau (1994) use the log of duration and the left-continuous version of the Kaplan–Meier estimate as specifications for $g(t_k)$ in cases where the distribution of duration has long tails.

Clearly, the specification of $g(t_k)$ is crucial, and yet Park and Hendry (2015) find that researchers often make arbitrary choices for $g(t_k)$, if they actually make a choice at all. This is indeed the case in Maeda's analysis of democratic breakdowns: Maeda estimates the model presented in Table 2 and implements the global test and covariate specific tests for nonproportionality in *Stata*. Maeda uses *Stata*'s default option for the timescale of the test, which is the identity function. Unfortunately, Maeda did not explore the alternative specifications for the function of time beyond this identity function, which is crucial because the correct selection of a timescale makes an important difference in test results.

While Grambsch and Therneau (1994) recommend the log of duration or the left-continuous Kaplan–Meier estimate when the distribution of time has long tails, Park and Hendry (2015) recommend that researchers consider three aspects of their data and research design: the level and pattern of censoring, the identification of censored and uncensored cases, and the presence of outliers. Based on simulations, Park and Hendry provide two sets of recommendations:

1. In the absence of outliers, untransformed duration may be used as the specification of $g(t_k)$. However, in the presence of outliers, $g(t_k)$ should use a transformation of duration. They argue that the rank transformation is often the best choice.
2. For low levels of censoring, the rank or the left-continuous Kaplan–Meier estimate transformations of $g(t_k)$ are often a better choice than the log of time. For high levels of censoring, the rank transformation outperforms alternative specifications.

2.4 Application: Nonproportionality in Democratic Breakdowns

From a practical perspective, the implementation of Grambsch and Therneau's test is relatively straightforward across software packages, and researchers can simply run all available versions of the timescale for $g(t_k)$. For instance, the call *cox.zph* in the *R* package *survival* offers multiple specifications for $g(t_k)$, including the identity function, the rank of event times, and the left-continuous version of the Kaplan–Meier estimate. Having said this, Table 3 presents multiple tests of nonproportional covariates. It is important to note that the results do not replicate the tests implemented by Maeda (2010), as the calculations in *Stata* and *R* are not the same. Nevertheless, the tests presented next do illustrate the mixed results that tests for nonproportionality may produce and the need for a thorough exploration of nonproportionality in applied settings.

Table 3 presents a mixed picture of the sources of nonproportionality. First, the global tests for the identity and rank timescales indicate that the model is proportional at the 95 percent confidence level. However, the test based on the Kaplan–Meier timescale indicates that there are nonproportional covariates. The individual scores across the three sets of tests also provide mixed evidence. Yet, at the 95 percent confidence level, all tests indicate that *Ethnic Fragmentation* is nonproportional.

Originally, Maeda (2010) finds that the covariates *Presidential System, Post–Cold War Era, Colony*, and *Regional Democracy Level* are not proportional at the 95 percent level. However, Maeda did not consider the alternative specifications of the timescale and ignored the weight of outliers with long democratic durations such as the USA and the UK. The presence of outliers indicates that the tests based on the rank timescale are better suited to identify nonproportional covariates. In this light, the evidence suggests that the effect of *Ethnic Fragmentation* on the hazard rate is not proportional.

Table 3 Test statistics of nonproportional covariates. Each column presents the χ^2 covariate-specific value of the test and its *p*-value in parentheses. Null hypothesis of proportional covariates. Tests produced by the following *R* code: phtest.id<-cox.zph(cox1,transform="identity", global=T) phtest.rnk<-cox.zph(cox1,transform="rank", global=T) phtest.km<-cox.zph(cox1,transform="km", global=T)

Variable	Identity	Rank	Kaplan–Meier
Development	1.8 (0.17)	1.7 (0.18)	2.8 (0.09)
Growth	1.0 (0.30)	1.5 (0.20)	2.8 (0.09)
Presidential System	2.9 (0.08)	2.9 (0.08)	2.8 (0.09)
Mixed System	0.3 (0.56)	0.0 (0.89)	0.6 (0.43)
Majority Government	0.2 (0.64)	0.0 (0.82)	0.0 (0.86)
Ethnic Fragmentation	4.8 (0.02)	6.0 (0.01)	7.8 (0.00)
Trade Openness	4.3 (0.03)	1.9 (0.16)	0.8 (0.35)
Urbanization	0.1 (0.67)	0.0 (0.83)	0.1 (0.69)
Post–Cold War Era	2.5 (0.11)	2.2 (0.13)	1.4 (0.22)
Imposed Policy	0.2 (0.62)	0.2 (0.63)	0.7 (0.37)
Colony	0.6 (0.41)	0.4 (0.49)	0.6 (0.43)
Military	0.3 (0.57)	0.1 (0.69)	0.2 (0.60)
Regional Democracy Level	0.8 (0.36)	1.3 (0.24)	3.4 (0.06)
Global Test	17.4 (0.18)	19.4 (0.11)	26.0 (0.01)

With confidence in the specification of the model, the recommended correction to nonproportional covariates indicates that the offending covariate should be interacted with a function of duration, often the natural logarithm of duration (e.g. Box-Steffensmeier & Jones, 2004). The corrected model is presented in Table 4.

The correction applied to *Ethnic Fragmentation* has had a significant statistical and substantive effect. In the original model, *Ethnic Fragmentation* did not have a statistically significant effect on the hazard rate. However, once the lack of proportionality was corrected and the specification was adjusted, the coefficients for both *Ethnic Fragmentation* and its interaction with the logarithm of duration are highly significant. Altogether, the substantive effect of ethnic fragmentation has changed considerably. As it will be demonstrated in the next section, results indicate that *Ethnic Fragmentation* decreases the hazard rate only in the early stages of a democracy. Once a democracy is more mature, the effect of ethnic fragmentation disappears. The techniques demonstrated in the next section describe how to interpret the effect of this type of covariate that has been adjusted to address lack of proportionality.

Table 4 Corrected Cox model of democratic breakdowns.
Unit: Democratic spell-month. Standard errors in
parentheses clustered at country level. Estimation results
produced by the following *R* code:

```
cox2new<-coxph(Surv(t0,t,d, type="counting",
    origin=0) ~ Zs + tethnic2, data=maeda,
    ties="efron", id=demid, cluster=country,
    robust=T, x=T)
```

Variable	Coefficient
Development	−0.6 (0.3)
Growth	−0.1 (0.0)
Presidential System	0.5 (0.7)
Mixed System	0.4 (0.9)
Majority Government	−0.7 (0.3)
Ethnic Fragmentation	−8.7 (2.8)
Trade Openness	−0.0 (0.0)
Urbanization	−0.0 (0.0)
Post–Cold War Era	−0.1 (0.5)
Imposed Policy	−0.0 (0.4)
Colony	−0.3 (0.7)
Military	−0.2 (0.4)
Regional Democracy Level	−0.1 (0.1)
Ln(t) (Ethnic Fragmentation)	2.1 (0.8)
Observations	28,468
Failures	42

2.5 Interpretation of Time-Varying Covariates

The previous section explains how to test for nonproportional covariates adequately. This is important because violating the proportionality assumption destroys the effectiveness of the Cox model. If testing is implemented correctly, then correcting nonproportional covariates by interacting them with a function of duration is relatively straightforward. However, this correction comes at the cost of increased complexity in the interpretation of substantive results, including the interpretation of coefficients, interactions over time, and the generation of quantities of interest. This section explores new techniques to understand the effect of corrections to nonproportional covariates and specifically the interaction of the offending covariate with a function of duration.

Consider again the Cox model with only one covariate Z and hazard rate $\lambda(t) = \lambda_0(t)\exp(Z\beta)$. If there is evidence that the effect of Z on the hazard rate is not proportional, the recommended correction produces the following specification: $\lambda(t) = \lambda_0(t)\exp(Z\beta_1 + \ln(t)Z\beta_2)$. Here, the nonproportional covariate Z is interacted with the natural logarithm of duration $\ln(t)$, thus creating the term $\ln(t)Z$. While this may be trivial, it is worth noting that the term $\ln(t)Z$ is time-varying by construction. This is relevant for two reasons. First, the corrected covariate should not be mistaken with other time-varying covariates, such as GDP per capita in Maeda's analysis (2010). These covariates vary over time but not because they have been interacted with duration. They should be predictable processes (Therneau & Grambsch, 2000: 5): "a process whose value at time t is known infinitesimally before t, at time $t-$, if not sooner." Second, statistical software may create interactions of nonproportional covariates with functions of time for convenience purposes, but researchers should be cautious that this automatic correction is not applied to proportional covariates.

The correction to nonproportional covariates mentioned previously is widely implemented in the social sciences. This correction has been applied to both single-record and multiple-record survival data, and while this does not present problems in a setting for multiple records, Jin and Boehmke (2017) find that the implementation of the correction in cases where covariates do not vary over time – for instance in single-record data – might introduce bias. Specifically, Jin and Boehmke (2017: 138) argue that "Including this interaction term means that the specification now involves time-varying covariates, and the model specification should reflect this feature." In other words, when researchers find nonproportional covariates in single-record data, they should expand the data and create multiple records where the duration of a unit is broken down into multiple observations. This expanded, multiple-record data should then be used to create the interaction of the offending covariate with a function of time. The R package *simPH* (Gandrud, 2015) can produce this type of extended data set.

Once a covariate is corrected and the interaction added to the model specification, researchers can compute multiple quantities of interest. One option is the term $Z\beta_1 + \ln(t)Z\beta_2$ in $\lambda_0(t)\exp(Z\beta_1 + \ln(t)Z\beta_2)$. This term is quite important because changes in Z in this function determine changes in the hazard rate; indeed, if the covariate Z is continuous, the marginal effect of Z on the function $Z\beta_1 + \ln(t)Z\beta_2$ is as follows:

$$\frac{\delta(Z\beta_1 + \ln(t)Z\beta_2)}{\delta Z} = \beta_1 + \ln(t)\beta_2. \tag{10}$$

This is sometimes known as a conditional linear coefficient (Licht, 2011). Using estimation results, the conditional linear coefficient may be transformed to a point estimate whose standard error may be calculated with the Delta method. If the covariate Z is discrete, researchers may focus on first differences.

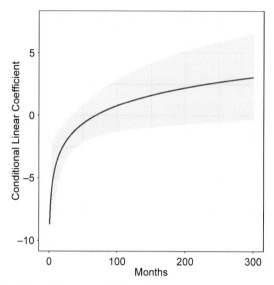

Figure 2 Conditional linear coefficient for *Ethnic Fragmentation*. Based on estimation results from the Cox model in Table 4. Ninety-five percent confidence interval in plum ribbon. Full *R* code is available at https://doi.org/10.7910/DVN/ADZUEA

All offending covariates should be corrected in this way, and therefore, there are as many relevant conditional linear coefficients as offending covariates.

The conditional linear coefficient may be interpreted with a graph that plots its values and confidence interval as a function of duration. Figure 2 presents a graph of the conditional linear coefficient for *Ethnic Fragmentation* according to the model in Table 4. The purple line is the estimate of the conditional linear coefficient and the plum ribbon around it is the 95 percent confidence interval.

As mentioned, conditional linear coefficients are important because they determine other quantities of interest. In particular, they reflect the contribution of covariates to the hazard rate. Therefore, it is useful to consider this coefficient in more detail. According to estimation results, the conditional linear coefficient for *Ethnic Fragmentation* is $-8.7 + 2.1\ln(t)$. For small values of duration, this coefficient is negative, but as duration increases, the coefficient becomes indistinguishable from zero. Thus, *Ethnic Fragmentation* decreases the hazard rate only in the early stages of a democracy, but as time goes by, the effect of ethnic fragmentation disappears.

The interpretation of corrected covariates has generated considerable debate in the social sciences mainly because the substantive effect of these variables changes over time by construction. For this reason, Licht (2011) developed a method to calculate two key quantities of interest in a corrected Cox model:

relative hazards and percent changes in the hazard rates, which are sometimes labeled as "first differences."

A relative hazard is a special case of the hazard ratio. In the previous example of Japan and Nepal, the ratio of their hazard rates is as follows:

$$\frac{\lambda_{\text{Japan}}(t)}{\lambda_{\text{Nepal}}(t)} = \frac{\lambda_0(t)\exp(\$49187\beta)}{\lambda_0(t)\exp(\$859\beta)} = \exp((\$49187-\$859)\beta) = \exp(\$48328\beta).$$

$$(11)$$

Equation (11) may be written as follows for a more general case:

$$\frac{\lambda_i(t)}{\lambda_{\neg i}(t)} = \frac{\lambda_0(t)\exp(Z_i\beta)}{\lambda_0(t)\exp(Z_{\neg i}\beta)} = \exp((Z_i - Z_{\neg i})(\beta)). \qquad (12)$$

In the context of the correction to nonproportionality, when a covariate Z is not proportional and its interaction with time is included in the specification, the hazard ratio is:

$$\frac{\lambda_i(t)}{\lambda_{\neg i}(t)} = \frac{\lambda_0(t)\exp(Z_i\beta_1 + \ln(t)Z_i\beta_2)}{\lambda_0(t)\exp(Z_{\neg i}\beta_1 + \ln(t)Z_{\neg i}\beta_2)} = \exp((Z_i - Z_{\neg i})(\beta_1 + \ln(t)\beta_2)). \quad (13)$$

The relative hazard version of this ratio assumes that $Z_{\neg i} = 0$, which yields:

$$\frac{\lambda_i(t)}{\lambda_{\neg i}(t)} = \exp((Z_i)(\beta_1 + \ln(t)\beta_2)). \qquad (14)$$

Likewise, the percentage change in a hazard rate for unit i relative to unit $\neg i$ is:

$$\%\Delta\lambda_i(t) = (\exp((Z_i - Z_{\neg i})(\beta_1 + \ln(t)\beta_2)) - 1) \times 100 \qquad (15)$$

Licht (2011) proposes a simulation-based method to compute these quantities, which she implements in *Stata* for a particular application. The simulation has now been developed for *R* by Gandrud (2015) and can be widely applied to Cox models; it can also be extended to polynomials and penalized splines of time. Figure 3 uses the package *simPH* to simulate the percent changes in the hazard rate as determined by *Ethnic Fragmentation* and its interaction with the logarithm of duration according to the results of the model of Table 4. The figure presents three ribbons of simulated values (Gandrud, 2015: 8): "The most transparent shows the furthest extent of the central or shortest probability interval. The less transparent ribbon shows the central 50 percent of this interval. And the middle line shows the interval's median."

The figure presents the percent change in a hazard rate as given by a change in *Ethnic Fragmentation*. The substantive effect confirms previous results from the conditional linear coefficient: in the early stages of a democracy, changes in *Ethnic Fragmentation* produce negative changes in the hazard rate, but as

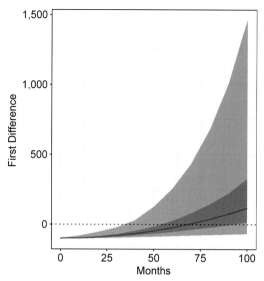

Figure 3 Simulated first difference for *Ethnic Fragmentation*. Based on estimation results from the Cox model in Table 4. Ribbons of simulated values with most transparent showing furthest extent of probability interval, less transparent showing 50 percent of probability interval, and solid line showing the median of the probability interval. Simulation results produced by the following *R* code: sim.cox2new <-coxsimtvc(obj=cox2new, b="ethnic", btvc="tethnic2", qi="First Difference", Xj=1, tfun="log", from=0, to=100, by=10) simGG(sim.cox2new, type="ribbons", lsize=1, legend=F, alpha=.3, xlab="Months")

the democracy matures and becomes more established, the effect of ethnic fragmentation disappears.

This approach to interpreting hazard rates in the context of nonproportional covariates is very useful for understanding substantive effects. It is important to note, however, that the quantities of interest are either relative hazards or percent changes in a hazard rate, which do not depend on the unknown "baseline" hazard $h_0(t)$, which drops out of the relevant terms in Eqs. (14) and (15). It is also important to note that the modeling and approach to the interpretation of covariates described previously is limited to hazard rates, which are short-term transition forces. Therefore, quantities of interest that look beyond hazard rates, such as cumulative incidence functions or transition probabilities, are not taken into consideration. In this light, it may be more relevant to understand the effect of a covariate on the probability that a unit will occupy a different state at some other point in time. These types of questions are ideal for multistate structures, which will be introduced in Section 5.

2.6 Summary

Researchers must test for a potential failure of the proportionality assumption in proportional models such as Cox or Weibull. Any covariate that has a nonproportional effect on the hazard rate must be corrected, and its substantive effect must be adequately interpreted. Before testing for nonproportional covariates, researchers must be confident that model specification and functional form are correct. Otherwise, Grambsch and Therneau's test may produce a false positive. At the same time, researchers must choose carefully the function of time used in the global test in order to obtain accurate evidence. Since these functions of time are easily implemented, researchers may use all available functions and look for consistent failures of the proportionality assumption. Once researchers have sufficient confidence in the results provided by Grambsch and Therneau's test, offending covariates may be corrected with an interaction with a function of duration. Once covariates are corrected, researchers have multiple options for interpretation of these time-varying covariates. While analytical results are useful, there are multiple graphical tools to evaluate the effect of time-varying covariates, including point estimates and standard errors of conditional linear coefficients as well as simulations of relative hazards or percent changes in a hazard rate.

2.7 Further Readings

The Element encourages readers to study Cox's article (1972) and Grambsch and Therneau's article on proportional hazards tests (1994). They constitute essential reading about the simplicity of the Cox model and the consequences of breaking the proportionality assumption. Over the past ten years, social scientists have further explored these concepts and provided key lessons, including Keele's (2010) work on specification and proportionality, Park and Hendry (2015) on the implementation of tests, as well as Jin and Boehmke (2017) on lack of proportionality in single-record data. Licht (2011) offers very useful techniques for the interpretation of time-varying covariates in survival analysis, while the *R* package *simPH* by Gandrud (2015) is a very practical tool to interpret these covariates in *R*.

3 Repeated Events

In models of single events, units experience the event of interest only once and never return to the risk set. In many social science applications, however, units experience repeated events. For instance, individuals have multiple periods of employment in a life time, and political leaders have multiple periods in office. These are examples of repeated events with single destinations. Indeed, the event that is experienced by the unit must be of the same type, such as different spells of democracy or multiple periods in political office. The difference with the mortality model described in the previous section is that events may be experienced multiple times, and therefore, units may enter and exit the risk repeatedly. Consider Maeda's analysis of democratic breakdowns (2010). In this case, the event of interest is the termination of a democratic spell.

Traditionally, multiple spells were assumed to be independent events. This approach is incorrect, as repeated spells are most likely correlated. In this light, a class of solutions known as variance-correction models adjusts the variance-covariance matrix to address the lack of independence in observations for the same unit. Alternatively, models may directly address dependence between events, for instance, by stratifying the hazard rate by event number. Today, researchers have access to many different types of models, from variance-correction to conditional frailty models to mixed models with random and fixed effects. It is worth noting that multistate models as well as event count processes may also be used for repeated events where researchers have the choice of modeling the number of repeated events rather than their durations.

3.1 A Review of Models for Repeated Events

For repeated events of the same type, there is a large menu of modeling options. Some of these models are well known, such as the variance-correction models. Other approaches such as mixed models with fixed and random effects have been developed recently. An overview of modeling options for repeated events is presented in Figure 4.

3.1.1 Variance-Correction Models

Variance-correction models (e.g. Box-Steffensmeier & Jones, 2004) adjust the variance-covariance matrix in order to address the lack of independence between observations for the same subject caused by the repeated events. As indicated by Therneau and Grambsch (2000), this is accomplished by clustering the standard errors by the unit at risk, which can be easily implemented across software platforms, often with a "cluster ()" option for particular calls or commands. It is important to note that all these models assume that the events of interest are ordered. For example, in the case of multiple spells of democracy, it is assumed that there is a first spell of democracy, a second spell of democracy, a third spell of democracy, and so on. These are ordered spells caused by ordered transitions.

The intuition behind the correction of the variance-covariance matrix is not that different from the correction applied to the variance-covariance matrix in

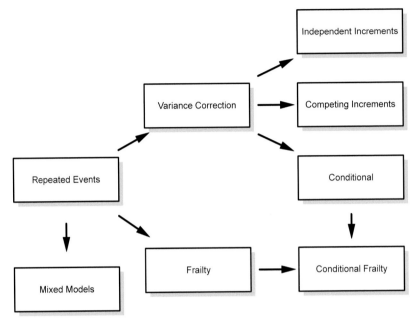

Figure 4 Models for repeated events

the linear model when observations do not meet the independence assumption. In survival analysis, the durations for different units are independent, but in repeated events, the same unit appears multiple times with different durations; these are the durations of the repeated events, and it is reasonable to assume that these spells are not independent from each other. Yet several analyses of duration fail to address this issue.

Consider the analysis of leader tenure in office, which often uses data from *Archigos*, a database of political leaders (Goemans, Gleditsch, & Chiozza, 2009). *Archigos* records multiple spells of tenure in office for individual leaders, such as De Gaulle in France, Andreotti in Italy, or Churchill in the UK. This is important information, but a popular approach assumes that these spells in office are independent, and therefore, the clustering is applied to countries and not to leaders. The intuition behind this approach is that observations for units that belong to a particular category, such as a country, are not independent. While this is convenient, it loses information unnecessarily if the objective is to model repeated events. For this reason, variance-correction models for repeated events cluster the standard errors by the unit at risk of experiencing multiple events.

Having said this, the three most popular variance-correction models for repeated events are the *Independent Increments*, *Competing Increments*, and

Table 5 Characteristics of three variance-correction models. Format of data adapted by permission from Springer Nature Customer Service Centre GmbH: Springer Nature, Modeling Survival Data: Extending the Cox Model by Therneau and Grambsch, 2000

	Independent Increments	Competing Increments	Conditional
Elapsed-time?	Yes	Yes	Yes
Gap-time?	Yes	Not often	Yes
Strata?	No	Yes	Yes
Format	Interval Stratum (0,7] 1 (7–33] 1 (33–60] 1	Interval Stratum (0,7] 1 (0–33] 2 (0–60] 3	Interval Stratum (0,7] 1 (7–33] 2 (33–60] 3

Conditional models. The independent increments model is also known as the Andersen–Gill model, while the competing increments model is also known as the Wei–Lin–Weissfeld or marginal model. According to Therneau and Grambsch (2000: 185): "All three are 'marginal' regression models in that $\hat{\beta}$ is determined from a fit that ignores the correlation [between durations for the same unit] followed by a corrected variance $D'D$, but differ considerably in their creation of the risks sets." Indeed, the risk set across models depends on the format of duration, which may be measured in elapsed-time or in gap-time. Additionally, some models stratify the number of events or transitions, which leads to the estimation of event-specific hazards. Table 5 presents the characteristics of the three models mentioned previously.

There are important similarities and differences between these models. First, all these models correct the variance-covariance matrix in order to address the lack of independence between observations for the same unit. Second, most models can accommodate duration in an elapsed-time format. This means that the models may use total duration since the unit first entered the risk set. Regardless of the data format used in repeated events models, it is crucial that researchers correctly set up the survival data, which will consist of multiple-record data, and carefully set the time intervals using start-stop codes and identification of the durations for the same unit.

Consider the following example for an elapsed-time format. Here, countries first enter the risk set of autocratic reversal when they become democracies. For simplicity, we can assume that countries are born democracies, and this is when they enter the risk set (of autocratic reversal) for the first time. Now assume that a particular country experiences a transition to autocracy in month 7. From then on, the country is no longer at risk because it is already an autocracy. After some time as an autocracy, the country becomes democratic, thus entering the risk set (of autocracy) for a second time. In this case, the country experiences a second event, that is, a second reversal to autocracy, in month 33. After spending a second period as an autocracy, the country rejoins the risk set only to be right-censored in month 60 when it is no longer under observation. Note that the country may have spent 300 months as an autocracy between the first and the second democratic spells. From an elapsed-time perspective, what matters is that the first democratic spell started in month 0 and ended in month 7, while the second spell started in month 7 of democracy and ended in month 33 even if the country spent 300 months as an autocracy between these spells. What matters, however, is that this country has been a democracy for a total of 33 months. In this light, the duration of the first democratic spell in elapsed-time is 7 months, and the duration of the second democratic spell in elapsed-time is 33 months. The competing increments model in Table 5 describes the data setup for elapsed-time.

The independent increments and conditional models may easily accommodate duration in gap-time. To avoid confusion, it might be better to refer to this format as restart-the-clock-time. In the previous example, this means that the duration of the first democratic spell is seven months, that is, $7 - 0 = 7$ months, and the duration for the second democratic spell is $33 - 7 = 26$ months. This restarts the clock for the second spell, which is a form of "renewal process" (Therneau & Grambsch, 2000). The conditional model in Table 5 describes this format for time.

Note, however, that the conditional model, as well as the independent increments model, can also use data in elapsed-time format. While researchers are therefore free to choose the format of the data in these two models, it is important that the decision is well justified and appropriate for the research question and the available data. For instance, a restart-the-clock-time format may be suitable for a country that experienced two democratic spells: one from 1857 to 1862 and one from 1997 to 2012, as the two periods of democracy may be too far apart from each other. However, if argued correctly, it is possible to analyze these two spells using an elapsed-time format.

Repeated events models differ widely in terms of approaches to stratification. The conditional and competing increments models stratify the baseline hazard rate by event number. In other words, each spell has its own baseline hazard. The conditional model in Table 5 presents a good example of the setup for stratification. In the previous example, this means that the baseline hazard for the

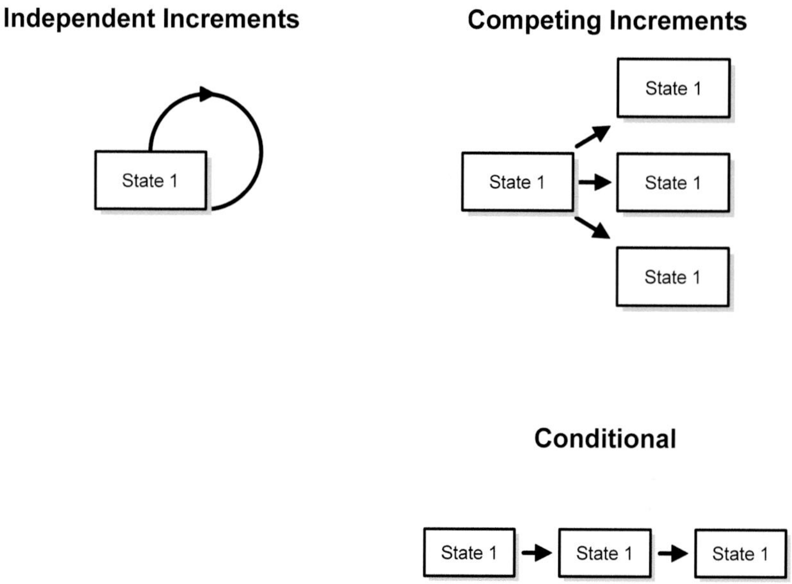

Independent Increments   **Competing Increments**

Conditional

Figure 5 Stratification in three variance-correction models. Adapted by permission from Springer Nature Customer Service Centre GmbH: Springer Nature, Modeling Survival Data: Extending the Cox Model by Therneau and Grambsch, 2000

first democratic period will be different to the baseline hazard for the second period and so on. However, the independent increments model assumes that the baseline hazards do not vary over the number of transitions, and therefore, the model does not stratify the baseline hazard. Technically, the only difference between the independent increments model and a traditional Cox model is that the former corrects the variance-covariance matrix. Figure 5 presents a visualization of the stratification of variance-correction models, where each arrow represents an event followed by a stratum (Therneau & Grambsch, 2000).

It is also important to note that the format for duration in the independent increments and the conditional models is identical. Indeed, both models very often rely on a restart-the-clock-time format where the duration for each spell is renewed. Both models also correct the variance-covariance matrix. The key difference between them is that the conditional model keeps track of the number of events and assumes that the baseline hazard differs over these events. To continue with the example of institutional change, in the conditional model, the baseline hazard for the fifth transition to autocracy is different from the first one and hence the need for stratification. In contrast, in the independent increments model, all transitions from democracy to autocracy are identical conditional on covariates.

3.2 Conditional Frailty Models

Frailty models approach repeated events from a different perspective: the correlation in multiple spells is caused by a form of unobserved heterogeneity that makes some units more prone to experience multiple events. In other words, if the heterogeneity could be observed, measured, and added to the specification, the correlation between observations for the same unit would disappear. According to Therneau and Grambsch (2000: 169): "The [frailty] model includes a random per-subject effect; multiple outcomes are assumed to be independent conditional on the per-subject coefficient."

Frailty models – often in its gamma version– are used in social sciences to model unobserved heterogeneity in the spirit of random effects rather than as a technique to analyze repeated events. Of course, issues of repeatability and heterogeneity are substantively interesting. For instance, there may be hidden covariates that explain why some leaders have multiple spells in office and others do not. If it was possible to model that heterogeneity, then we could have more confidence in approaches that assume that politicians' multiple spells in office are independent. But even if such heterogeneity could be modeled, it is substantively important to understand which observed variables help us understand why some leaders have multiple spells in office and why some spells are longer than others.

Box-Steffensmeier, De Boef, and Joyce (2007) present an excellent discussion of the advantages and disadvantages of variance-correction models, frailty models, and models that combine variance-correction with unobserved heterogeneity. The starting point is that variance-correction models could indirectly address heterogeneity by correcting the variance-covariance matrix: "Yet in all cases, because the variance-corrected models do not incorporate the heterogeneity directly at the estimation stage, the estimates remain biased" (Box-Steffensmeier, De Boef, & Joyce, 2007: 240). Pure frailty models experience other types of problems, including the selection of the family for the frailty term, the potential lack of independence between the frailty and the covariates, and the absence of stratification and consequently the inability to model event-specific hazards.

In this context, researchers may estimate a conditional frailty model to simultaneously address event dependence and unobserved heterogeneity. According to Box-Steffensmeier, De Boef, and Joyce (2007: 238): "simulation evidence indicates that the conditional frailty model is superior to alternative models when repeated event processes are characterized by both event dependence and heterogeneity." The conditional frailty model, estimated via a Cox model, has the following hazard rate:

$$\lambda_{ik}(t) = \lambda_{0k}(t - t_{k-1}) \exp(Z_{ik}\beta + \omega_i). \tag{16}$$

Here Z is a matrix of covariates and ω is a vector of unknown random effects by individual. Importantly, k is the event number, which allows for stratified baseline hazards, which is a key feature of the conditional frailty model. The model restarts the duration clock after each transition. The key to frailty models is the estimation of the variance of the vector of unknown random effects, often represented by θ. If this variance is close to zero, there is no heterogeneity in the process.

In the traditional frailty model, the vector ω is drawn from a gamma or a Gaussian distribution, although most work focuses on draws from the gamma distribution. It is important to note that frailty models can be estimated as penalized Cox models, which are computationally convenient (Therneau & Grambsch, 2000). In fact, a Cox model with penalty $p(\omega) = (1/\theta) \sum (\omega_i - \exp(\omega_i))$ is equivalent to a Gamma frailty model. For the Gaussian model, the penalty is $p(\omega) = (1/2\theta) \sum \omega_i^2$. Both penalized Cox models assume that $\omega_1, \omega_2, ... \omega_q$ are a random sample from the relevant distribution. Specifically for the gamma model, it is assumed that the ω_i are logs of independent and identically distributed gamma random variables.

3.2.1 Mixed Models

Therneau (2020) has developed a mixed effects Cox model with fixed and random effects. Nested in this model is the traditional frailty model. It is worth noting that this mixed effects models refers to fixed effects as the systematic part of a model (e.g. $Z\beta$) rather than the unit-specific effects often used in the context of the linear model. The advantage of the mixed effects model is that it can estimate the vector ω of random effects as draws from a Gaussian distribution. Additionally, the standard deviation from the random effect is directly interpretable and the model can be extended to correlated random effects using a kingship matrix, which provides a measure of closeness among individuals, often family members in clinical settings. The mixed effects model for survival analysis is implemented by the package *coxme* and follows the notation for mixed models in *R*.

3.3 Democratic Breakdowns as Repeated Events

In order to analyze democratic breakdowns from a perspective of repeated events, the unit of analysis used in previous sections needs to be replaced. In Maeda's work (2010), the unit of analysis is the democratic spell-month. Maeda acknowledges the lack of independent observations caused by unobserved heterogeneity, which he addresses by clustering the standard errors by country. Moreover, he includes in the specification a variable for the number of times that a country has experienced a democratic breakdown, which turned out to be statistically insignificant and was therefore eliminated from Maeda's reported specifications. While these are convenient corrections, this approach does not really tackle the repeated nature of democratic spells by country – this requires that the unit of analysis changes from the democratic spell-month to the country-month. Only then is it possible to stratify a model using the repeated spells of democracy while modeling other aspects of the risk set such as the format for duration. To be clear, the analysis of repeated democratic spells was not Maeda's goal, which focuses on different types of democratic breakdowns in a context of competing risks.

Having said this, recall that in Maeda's (2010) data set there are 108 countries and 141 democratic spells. Seventy-two countries do not experience repeated spells of democracy, while 28 countries have 2 spells, 7 countries have 3 spells, and 1 country, Turkey, has 4 spells of democracy. Altogether, there are only 45 breakdowns of democracy. In the analyses that follow, the unit of analysis is the country-month. Table 6 presents independent increments, conditional, and conditional frailty models, as well as a mixed effects model. Estimation is based on the model of Table 4 that corrects the lack of proportionality in the effect of *Ethnic Fragmentation* on the hazard rate.

The substantive results from specific variables across models are very similar, and they all indicate an absence of heterogeneity. In the conditional frailty model, the estimate of θ is very close to zero, and its χ^2 test is 0.0 with a p-value of 0.9. Moreover, the log likelihoods for the conditional and the conditional frailty models are almost identical, and their likelihood ratio test indicates that there is no difference between them. The mixed effects model with Gaussian frailty confirms an absence of heterogeneity. The log likelihood of the mixed model is -141.24, and the log likelihood for the null model is -141.55, which are very similar. The likelihood ratio test for these two models indicates that there is no difference between them.

This notwithstanding, it is worth discussing the results of the mixed model, as it is a new addition to repeated events techniques. The model estimates an intercept effect per country – if these countries have the same intercept, this means that there is no variance and therefore no heterogeneity. Large variance in the group effects suggests the presence of heterogeneity, although in this particular case it does not make a difference. Estimation results present a random intercept effect per country with a standard deviation of 0.51, which means that the relative risk for countries in this category is 67 percent higher (i.e. $\exp(0.51) = 1.67$).

Table 6 Cox models of repeated democratic spells. Unit: Country-month. Standard errors in parentheses clustered at country level. Full R code is available at https://doi.org/10.7910/DVN/ADZUEA

Variable	Ind. Increments	Conditional	Conditional Frailty	Mixed Model
Development	−0.7 (0.3)	−0.7 (0.3)	−0.7 (0.3)	−0.7 (0.3)
Growth	−0.1 (0.0)	−0.1 (0.0)	−0.1 (0.0)	−0.1 (0.0)
Presidential System	0.4 (0.7)	0.5 (0.6)	0.5 (0.6)	0.5 (0.6)
Mixed System	0.3 (1.0)	0.4 (0.8)	0.4 (0.7)	0.4 (0.7)
Majority Gov.	−0.7 (0.3)	−0.6 (0.3)	−0.6 (0.4)	−0.6 (0.4)
Ethnic Fragmentation	−4.2 (2.5)	−8.0 (3.5)	−8.0 (3.1)	−4.7 (2.5)
Trade Openness	−0.0 (0.0)	−0.0 (0.0)	−0.0 (0.0)	−0.0 (0.0)
Urbanization	−0.0 (0.0)	−0.0 (0.0)	−0.0 (0.0)	−0.0 (0.0)
Post–Cold War Era	−0.2 (0.5)	−0.2 (0.5)	−0.2 (0.6)	−0.1 (0.5)
Imposed Policy	−0.1 (0.4)	−0.0 (0.4)	−0.0 (0.5)	−0.3 (0.6)
Colony	−0.5 (0.9)	−0.1 (0.7)	−0.1 (0.6)	−0.4 (0.6)
Military	−0.1 (0.5)	−0.2 (0.5)	−0.2 (0.5)	−0.0 (0.5)
Reg. Dem. Level	−0.1 (0.1)	−0.1 (0.1)	−0.1 (0.1)	−0.1 (0.1)
Ln(t) (Ethnic Frag.)	0.9 (0.6)	1.9 (0.9)	1.9 (0.8)	1.0 (0.6)
Variance θ			$5e - 09$	0.26
Observations	28,468	28,468	28,468	28,468
Failures	42	42	42	42
Log-L	−141.55	−117.57	−117.57	−141.24

In light of this evidence, and particularly given the absence of heterogeneity, the conditional model provides very useful information about the role of stratification. Hazard rates are difficult to produce after the estimation of repeated events models. Yet cumulative hazards are available after estimation, and they provide an indication of the accumulation of risk as determined by the area under the hazard rate. Figure 6 presents an estimate of the cumulative hazard function for four countries: Mexico (1997–2004), Argentina (1973–2004), Sudan (1954–1989), and Turkey (1946–2004). These are interesting cases because they have one, two, three, and four spells of democracy, respectively.

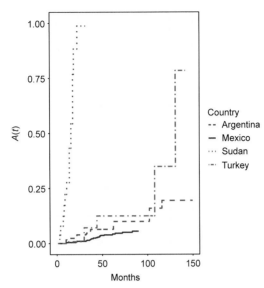

Figure 6 Estimated cumulative hazard functions. Based on estimation results from the conditional model in Table 6 using covariate values from Mexico (1997–2004), Argentina (1973–2004), Sudan (1954–1989), and Turkey (1946–2004). Predictions for the figure were produced by the following *R* code: cox.cond <- coxph(Surv(elapt0,elapt,d, type="counting", origin=0) ~ Zs + tethnic2 + strata(str), data=maeda, ties="efron", id=ccode, cluster=ccode, robust=T, x=T) four<-rbind(mex.rep, arg.rep, sud.rep, tur.rep) plot.cox.cond.all<-survfit(cox.cond, newdata=four, id=ccode, se.fit=F)

In other words, for the data available, Mexico has only one spell of democracy, while Argentina, Sudan, and Turkey have multiple spells.

In order to interpret cumulative hazards, it is useful to consider the rate of change in the cumulative hazard under a constant hazard rate. In this case, the accumulation of the area under the hazard rate over time should follow a constant rate. Deviations from this steady rate of accumulation give an indication, however imperfect, of how steep the hazard rate is.

Having said this, Figure 6 shows an interesting variation in the risk of autocratic transition across countries. Mexico, the only country that has not experienced multiple spells of democracy, presents a rather flat cumulative hazard, perhaps indicating that the hazard rate decreases over time. For the other countries with more fragile democracies, the risk of autocratic transition only begins to accumulate quickly late in a democratic period, with the exception of Sudan, which shows a rapid increase in the accumulation of risk.

3.4 Summary

From incarceration to democratization, many questions in the social sciences involve repeated events. For these reasons, models for repeated events are widely used by researchers. Yet the terminology of models and their specific setup in terms of the format of time and the use of stratification is sometimes confusing. Indeed, repeated models go well beyond the simple clustering of standard errors and involve the modeling of the potential causes of repeated events.

Models for repeated events are very flexible and can accommodate a number of approaches to our understanding of repeated spells. However, the mechanism behind repeated events is often seen as a nuisance that goes away with the addition of a frailty term as a measure of unobserved heterogeneity. This approach does not contribute to our understanding of repeated events. Instead, researchers must choose models and duration formats carefully in order to obtain relevant insight as produced by stratification and the modeling of heterogeneity as the cause of repeated spells. As demonstrated in this section, these two approaches are not mutually exclusive. Moreover, the Element encourages researchers to explore new models for fixed and random effects as a useful alternative to repeated spells.

3.5 Further Readings

Therneau and Grambsch (2000) present an excellent coverage of traditional models of repeated events. Box-Steffensmeier, De Boef, and Joyce (2007) discuss the advantages and disadvantages of these models and present, in detail, the conditional frailty model. The *R* package *survival* gives many useful details on how to estimate models for repeated events and particularly the use of multirecord data and time-varying covariates for prediction. The package *coxme* by Therneau (2020) is a recent development in the estimation of mixed models for repeated events, including mixed models with draws from a Gaussian distribution for the frailty, among other advanced techniques for unobserved heterogeneity.

4 Competing Risks

Competing risks models are some of the simplest, nontrivial multistate models. They are used widely in the social sciences, and therefore, this section does not discuss the details of basic estimation procedures. Instead, it elaborates on some aspects of these models that remain elusive, particularly a more nuanced use of Kaplan–Meier and Nelson–Aalen estimates of the survivor and cumulative hazard functions. In this context, the section introduces cumulative incidence functions as key quantities of interest in multistate models that address a bias caused by the artificial censoring of units in traditional competing risks models.

4.1 Characteristics of Competing Risks Models

The section now introduces some additional notation. Consider a duration process with three states labeled 1, 2, and 3. Assume that state 1 is the initial state. In the running example of democratic breakdowns, the initial state is democracy, which may be terminated by exogenous (state 2) or endogenous causes (state 3). In this case, there are two potential transitions from state 1, each with its own transition force or hazard rate. The first type of transition is from state 1 to state 2, with cause-specific hazard rate $\lambda_{12}(t)$. The second type of transition is from state 1 to state 3, with cause-specific hazard rate $\lambda_{13}(t)$. As mentioned previously, these hazard rates are also known as cause-specific hazard rates, or cause-specific transition forces, because they can be interpreted as the causes that pull a unit out of its initial state.

The two transition forces $\lambda_{12}(t)$ and $\lambda_{13}(t)$ together pull the unit out of the initial state 1, and therefore, the "all-cause" hazard rate from state 1 is $\lambda_{1.}(t) = \lambda_{12}(t) + \lambda_{13}(t)$. Likewise, there are two cumulative hazard rates $\Lambda_{12}(t) = \int_0^t \lambda_{12}(u)du$ and $\Lambda_{13}(t) = \int_0^t \lambda_{13}(u)du$, with the "all-cause" cumulative hazard rate $\Lambda_{1.}(t) = \Lambda_{12}(t) + \Lambda_{13}(t)$. It is important to note that these relationships hold under the assumption of independent competing risks. These transition forces are illustrated in Figure 7.

As mentioned in Section 1, survival analysis has focused mostly on the modeling of hazard rates. Hazard rates are short-term forces that pull units away from particular states, and they are crucial because they help us understand the determinants of immediate transitions and therefore the drivers of duration. In addition, hazard rates are the building blocks of more complex quantities of interest that focus on long-term aspects of a duration process. Indeed, rather than investigating why some factors, such as the state of the economy, pull

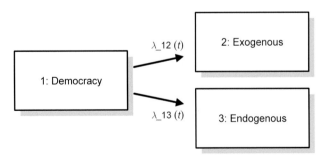

Figure 7 Democratic breakdowns and competing risks

away a country from democratic conditions toward more autocratic ones, it may be more relevant to know the probability that a country will continue to be a democracy given that it has been a democracy for seventy years. Likewise, we can ask what is the probability that a democracy will be an autocracy in, say, three years. These type of questions about long-term transition probabilities are ideal for multistate models (Hougaard, 2000), and competing risks are a special case of a multistate structure. In fact, competing risks models focus on a special case of transition probabilities: cumulative incidence functions.

4.2 The Importance of Cumulative Incidence Functions

In order to "make the transition" from hazard rates to cumulative incidence functions, it is necessary to briefly recall a popular approach to competing risks. In this approach, and as long as the risks are independent, researchers can estimate a separate model for each risk k in the competing risk set. If there are k risks, this leads to k models, each with its own survivor function $S_k(t)$. This is a very special survivor function where failures for causes different from k are right-censored. To be more precise, there is a cause-specific hazard rate $\lambda_k(t)$ for risk k, which can then be used to produce $\Lambda_k(t) = \int_0^t \lambda_k(u)du$, and a cause-specific survivor function $S_k(t) = \exp(-\Lambda_k(t))$. The complement of this survivor function is $1 - S_k(t)$.

Now consider the function $S(t) = \exp(-\sum_{k=1}^K \Lambda_k(t))$, where $S(t)$ is not subscripted. Putter, Fiocco, and Geskus (2007) note that $S_k(t)$ and $S(t)$ are very different: $S_k(t)$ is a naïve Kaplan–Meier estimator based on data where failures for causes different from k are right-censored, while $S(t)$ accounts for all failures. In the running example, Maeda focuses on the duration of 141 democratic spells. In this data, there is a total of 45 transitions from democracy to autocracy. Twenty-four of those transitions are exogenous, while 21 are endogenous. In this case, the relevant $S(t)$ for all transitions has 45 events, but for $S_{\text{exogenous}}(t)$, there are 24 events, while for $S_{\text{endogenous}}(t)$, there are 21 events. Indeed, the naïve $S_{\text{exogenous}}(t)$ and $S_{\text{endogenous}}(t)$ are based on an artificial transformation of the censoring indicators.

Having said this, the cumulative incidence function, $I_k(t)$, is the probability $P(T \leq t, D = k)$ of failing from cause k before and including time t, and it is defined as follows (Putter, Fiocco, & Geskus, 2007):

$$I_k(t) = \int_0^t \lambda_k(u)S(u)du. \tag{17}$$

Note that $I_k(t)$ uses $S(t)$, which is not subscripted. The cumulative incidence function is also known as the sub-distribution function, and it resembles the CDF due to Eq. (6) but with a key difference. According to Putter, Fiocco, and

Geskus (2007: 2398), "The [sub-distribution function] name has its origins in the fact that the cumulative probability to fail from cause k remains below one, $I_k(\infty) = P(D = k)$, hence it is not a proper probability distribution."

Now compare the naïve complement of this survivor function $1 - S_k(t)$ with the cumulative incidence function $I_k(t)$: $I_k(t)$ uses $S(t)$, while $1 - S_k(t)$ evidently uses $S_k(t)$. Putter, Fiocco, and Geskus (2007: 2399) argue that this difference is essential: "Since $S(t) \leq S_k(t)$, then $I_k(t) \leq 1 - S_k(t)$." This suggests that there is a form of bias in the naïve estimator $1 - S_k(t)$ that emerges from the artificial censoring of units that do not fail for the right reason in a competing risks model. Indeed, $S(t)$ is less than or equal to $S_k(t)$ simply because there are more failures in a survivor function that ignores the types of failures.

4.3 Competing Risks and Democratic Breakdowns

As an application of cumulative incidence functions, consider Maeda's (2010) competing risks analysis of democratic breakdowns. Maeda argues that a democratic government may be terminated by forces outside government – such as a coup – and by democratic leaders that end the democratic process itself – such as suspending a constitution. These two types of terminations are labeled exogenous and endogenous, respectively. The data set has 108 countries with 141 democratic spells. For this sample, there are only 45 breakdowns of democracy, with 24 exogenous terminations and 21 endogenous ones. Figure 8 presents nonparametric estimates of the cumulative incidence functions for these two types of risks.

Maeda approaches competing risks from a traditional perspective, that is, he estimates two separate Cox models, one for each risk, while right-censoring the spells that experience the competing risk. This section follows a different approach: rather than estimating two separate models, it uses the *R* package *survival* to estimate them jointly. *This does not make a difference on the substantive effect of the covariates on the cause-specific hazard rates*, and therefore, coefficients can be interpreted directly or as hazard ratios. The difference is that joint estimation facilitates the computation of cumulative incidence functions. The latter cannot be estimated under two separate models, as they artificially right-censor the cases experiencing competing risks, thus falling into the trap of using the naïve complement $1 - S_k(t)$. If the emphasis is on CDFs, models need to be estimated jointly: the substantive effects of covariates on cause-specific hazard rates are identical as estimating two separate models, but this format correctly estimates incidence functions.

Whether researchers choose to estimate separate or joint models of competing risks, they must test for a violation of the proportionality assumption.

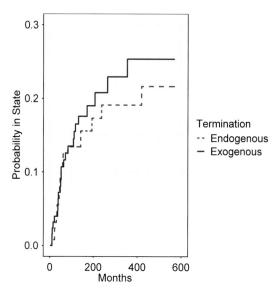

Figure 8 Cumulative incidence functions for types of democratic breakdowns. Estimates from the empirical Aalen–Johansen estimator. Estimates were produced by the following *R* code:

```
curves.mrec.comp<-survfit(Surv(t0,t,status,
type="counting", origin=0) ~ 1, id=demid, data=maeda).
```

Note that the censoring indicator `status` is a factor.

Tests for nonproportional covariates indicate that *Growth*, *Ethnic Fragmentation*, *Trade Openness*, and *Post-Cold War Era* are not proportional in the model of exogenous terminations, while *Presidential System* is not proportional in the model of endogenous terminations. Table 7 presents joint estimates from models that correct these nonproportional covariates.

As mentioned previously, results of Table 7 can be interpreted from a traditional perspective where coefficients reflect changes to the cause-specific hazards. These results may be used to generate conditional linear coefficients directly from estimation results or first differences based on simulation. However, this Element makes a case for the use and interpretation of alternative quantities of interest, such as cumulative incidence functions. Figure 9 presents predicted cumulative incidence functions from the estimation results of the corrected model in Table 7. All predictions in multistate models, including competing risks models, need covariate values. In this light, this section uses the values for all covariates for the end of the first democratic spell of Argentina in 1976. This democratic spell ends in month thirty-seven and is associated with particular covariate values for that month, all of which have been used for the prediction of cumulative incidence functions. The figure presents two

Table 7 Competing risks models of types of democratic breakdowns. Unit: Democratic spell-month. Standard errors in parentheses clustered at country level. Estimation results produced by the following R code: `corr.cox3and5` `<- coxph(list(Surv(t0,t,status, type="counting", origin=0)` `~ Zs, 1:2  tgro2 + tethnic2 + tope2 + tpostcw2, 1:3` `tpresi2), data=maeda, ties="efron", id=demid,` `cluster=country, robust=T, x=T`. Note that the censoring indicator status is a factor

Variable	Exogenous	Endogenous
Development	−0.7 (0.3)	−0.8 (0.4)
Growth	0.2 (0.2)	−0.0 (0.0)
Presidential System	−0.1 (1.2)	−6.2 (2.3)
Mixed System	−1.7 (2.3)	3.2 (1.0)
Majority Government	−0.6 (0.6)	−0.7 (0.3)
Ethnic Fragmentation	−8.3 (3.7)	−1.9 (1.3)
Trade Openness	−0.0 (0.0)	−0.0 (0.0)
Urbanization	−0.0 (0.0)	−0.0 (0.0)
Post–Cold War Era	−4.0 (4.6)	0.3 (1.0)
Imposed Policy	−0.6 (0.6)	1.1 (0.7)
Colony	−1.2 (0.8)	2.0 (1.0)
Military	0.2 (0.6)	−1.2 (1.0)
Regional Democracy Level	−0.2 (0.1)	0.0 (0.1)
Ln(t) (Growth)	−0.1 (0.0)	
Ln(t) (Ethnic Fragmentation)	2.0 (1.2)	
Ln(t) (Trade Openness)	−0.0 (0.0)	
Ln(t) (Post–Cold War Era)	0.9 (1.0)	
Ln(t) (Presidential System)		2.3 (0.7)
Observations	28,468	
Failures	42	

functions: one for a case of exogenous termination and one for endogenous ones.

4.3.1 Fine and Gray's Model

The estimates from Table 7 can be used to analyze the effects of covariates on cause-specific hazards. However, they cannot be used to explore the effects of covariates on cumulative incidence functions (Fine & Gray, 1999). Indeed, while covariate effects on hazard rates may be directly analyzed from the separate or joint estimation of models, it is wrong to infer that these effects will

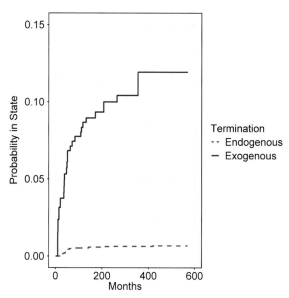

Figure 9 Predicted cumulative incidence functions for types of democratic breakdowns. Based on estimation results from the competing risks model of Table 7 using covariate values from democratic spell in Argentina in March 1976. Estimates from the Aalen–Johansen estimator. Estimates were produced by the following *R* code: `plot.corr.cox3and5 <-survfit(corr.cox3and5, newdata=arg1976.cr, se.fit=T)`

also apply to the incidence function, which is a complex, nonlinear function of cause-specific hazards and survivor functions. To fill this gap, Fine and Gray proposed a proportional hazards model for the sub-distribution of risks in order to analyze the effect of covariates on cumulative incidence functions.

Consider a competing risks model with k independent risks. In the running example of democratic breakdowns, there are $k = 2$ risks, one for exogenous terminations and one for endogenous ones. In this particular application, the goal is to model the cumulative incidence function $F_1(t, \mathbf{Z}) = P(T \leq t, k = 1 | \mathbf{Z})$ for risk 1, exogenous terminations. This is the same cumulative incidence function $I_k(t)$ denoted previously but conditional on covariates $\mathbf{Z}$.

The challenge in competing risks models is that the occurrence of event $k = 1$ precludes the occurrence of some other event $k \neq 1$. In the running example, the occurrence of an exogenous termination precludes the occurrence of an endogenous one. However, Fine and Gray (1999) use this information to define an improper random variable T^* such that:

$$T^* = I(k = 1) \times T + (1 - I(k = 1)) \times \infty. \tag{18}$$

This is an important understanding of the sub-distribution of risk k. We observe the duration of units that experience the risk $k = 1$. For those units that would have experienced $k = 1$ but instead experienced event $k \neq 1$, the duration is infinite. This will play a key role in the practical implementation of Fine and Gray's model in R.

Having said this, the improper random variable has the following sub-distribution hazard (Fine & Gray, 1999):

$$\lambda_1(t, \mathbf{Z}) = \lim_{\Delta t \to 0} \frac{Pr(t \leq T \leq t + \Delta t, k = 1 | T \geq t \cup (T \leq t \cap k \neq 1), \mathbf{Z})}{\Delta t}. \quad (19)$$

This is a key term, as it denotes the sub-distribution hazard as a quantity that is conditional on the occurrence of risk $k = 1$ for $T \geq t$ or the occurrence of another risk $k \neq 1$ for $T \leq t$.

Now, recall that a hazard rate is the ratio of the PDF and the survivor function, both of which can be expressed as functions of the CDF. After some calculus and some rearrangement, the sub-distribution hazard is:

$$\lambda_1(t, \mathbf{Z}) = \frac{-d \log(1 - F_1(t, \mathbf{Z}))}{dt} \quad (20)$$

Fine and Gray (1999) show that if $g(F_1(t, \mathbf{Z}))$ is any known, increasing function, and in particular for $g = \log(-\log(1 - u))$, then:

$$F_1(t, \mathbf{Z}) = 1 - \exp(- \int_0^t \lambda_{10}(u) \exp(\mathbf{Z}\beta) du), \quad (21)$$

where $\lambda_{10}(t) \exp(\mathbf{Z}\beta)$ are the components of a hazard rate $\lambda_1(t, \mathbf{Z})$, which is assumed to be proportional.[4]

The practical implementation of Fine and Gray's model (1999) relies on the improper random variable T^*. As mentioned, the sub-distribution mechanism for risk $k = 1$ states that $T^* = \infty$ when a unit experiences the competing event $k \neq 1$. In this light, in order to model the cumulative incidence function of risk $k = 1$, the *survival* package in R artificially extends the duration of units that experience the event $k \neq 1$ in order to keep those units in the risk set for $k = 1$. The method technically creates a new data set for each risk with observed durations for units that experience $k = 1$ and with artificial durations for units that experience the event $k \neq 1$. Clearly, the artificial durations are created for time periods after the units experience the event $k \neq 1$. The method also produces weights for these artificial durations, which are then used in estimation of the sub-distribution hazard. In this approach, *estimation of the effects of covariates on the cumulative incidence function for risk $k = 1$* relies on a weighted Cox proportional hazards model that uses the new data set as the estimation sample. This is then repeated for each risk $k \neq 1$. While this method is relatively

---

[4] Note that $F_1(t, \mathbf{Z})$ is written as $1 - S(t)$, where $S(t)$ is written as a function of the cumulative hazard as shown in Eq. (5).

Table 8 Fine and Gray's model applied to democratic breakdowns. Unit: Democratic spell-month. Standard errors in parentheses clustered at country level. Full R code is available at https://doi.org/10.7910/DVN/ADZUEA

Variable	Exogenous	Endogenous
Development	−0.5 (0.3)	−0.6 (0.4)
Growth	−0.1 (0.0)	−0.0 (0.0)
Presidential System	−0.6 (0.8)	−5.1 (3.0)
Mixed System	−1.4 (1.3)	3.0 (1.0)
Majority Government	−0.6 (0.6)	−0.5 (0.4)
Ethnic Fragmentation	−0.0 (1.0)	−1.7 (1.3)
Trade Openness	−0.0 (0.0)	−0.0 (0.0)
Urbanization	−0.0 (0.0)	−0.0 (0.0)
Post–Cold War Era	−0.3 (0.7)	0.8 (0.9)
Imposed Policy	−1.2 (0.9)	1.3 (0.8)
Colony	−8.0 (2.7)	2.0 (1.0)
Military	0.5 (0.6)	−1.6 (1.0)
Regional Democracy Level	−0.2 (0.1)	0.0 (0.1)
Ln(t) (Colony)	1.7 (0.6)	
Ln(t) (Presidential System)		2.0 (0.7)
Observations	28,672	28,650
Failures	24	18

complex and not without weaknesses, research in biostatistics shows that Fine and Gray's model is superior to the naïve Cox model in accurately assessing the incidence of events.

Table 8 presents estimation results from Fine and Gray's model (1999) of the sub-distribution applied to Maeda's competing risks setup of types of democratic breakdowns.

Coefficients and hazard ratios from estimation results in Fine and Gray's model reflect covariate effects on the respective cumulative incidence function. For instance, the coefficients in column 2 reflect the effect of covariates on the incidence of an exogenous termination; negative coefficients indicate a reduction in the incidence, while positive ones reflect an increase. It is important to note that covariate effects on the incidence function might be very different from covariate effects on the hazard rate, as discussed previously. For instance, *Colony* does not have a significant effect on the hazard rate of exogenous terminations, as indicated by the estimation results of Table 7. However, results from Fine and Gray's model indicate that both *Colony* and its interaction with the logarithm of duration have highly significant effects on the cumulative incidence of exogenous terminations. Given the signs and magnitudes of their coefficients, it is safe to say that *Colony* reduces the incidence of exogenous terminations for early durations.

4.4 Summary

In the traditional approach to competing risks, researchers estimate separate event history models for each risk. As long as the risks are independent, this is an appropriate technique. However, it is important that researchers interpret coefficients carefully and compute the relevant quantities of interest. For instance, estimating k models for k risks will result in coefficient estimates for the cause-specific hazard rates. This is perfectly fine if the emphasis is on hazard analysis, which faces familiar obstacles in the diagnosis of nonproportional covariates and the interpretation of time-varying covariates, as discussed previously.

An analysis of transition probabilities will complement traditional competing risks models. This approach focuses on the likelihood that a unit will occupy a particular state at some point in time. In this light, rather than exploring the effects of covariates on the forces that pull a unit toward one destination, the focus is on the probability that a unit will end up in that destination. This requires an analysis of cumulative incidence functions. While researchers may compute this quantity manually, it is recommended that they estimate models for each risk jointly, as demonstrated in this section. This can be followed by an estimation of Fine and Gray's model, which, while imperfect (Therneau, Crowson, & Atkinson, 2021), will shed light on the effect of covariates on cumulative incidence functions.

4.5 Further Readings

Social scientists have fully embraced the traditional approach to modeling competing risks. At the same time, there has been considerable progress in the development of competing risks, particularly in the area of cumulative incidence functions and subdistributions. Beyersmann, Allignol, and Schumacher's *Competing Risks and Multistate Models with R* (2012) is an excellent and modern overview of competing risks that serves as a gate to more complex multistate models. Haller, Schmidt, and Ulm (2013) present a useful summary of developments in biostatistics, the field where the most advanced techniques in competing risks are developed. Therneau, Crowson, and Atkinson's "Multistate models and competing risks" (2021) vignette for the implementation of multistate models and competing risks in R, including Fine and Gray's model (1999), is also a key reference for the estimation of competing risks models.

5 Multistate Models

Multistate models are the most general form of survival processes. Mortality and competing risks models, among others, are special cases of multistate structures. More complex types of processes, such as a mix of competing risks and alternating events, can also be analyzed from a multistate perspective. For instance, pairs of rival countries may go directly into battle, or they may experience first an international crisis and then a battle, or they may de-escalate the crisis and go back to the status quo. This is a particular application of the illness-death multistate model depicted in Figure 1 where units are allowed to enter and exit transition states multiple times until they reach an absorbing state. This model can be extended to address situations where units go back and forth between states without ever reaching an absorbing state. This is a particularly useful structure for the analysis of democratic transitions and autocratic reversals where countries never settle into a stable democracy or autocracy and for a very large period of time they go back and forth between these two types of regimes.

Multistate models facilitate the analysis of very complex survival structures. Indeed, they allow for situations where there may not be an initial state or where all states are transitioning states or even where there are repeated competing risks. Multistate models often focus on the estimation of transition probabilities where the quantity of interest is the probability that a unit will occupy a particular state l at some time t given that it is in a different state m at some time $v \neq t$.

These models have been used in biostatistics for more than twenty years (e.g. Borgan, 1997; Hougaard, 2000), and social scientists recently introduced them to social science applications (e.g. Metzger & Jones, 2016). This section further promotes the use of multistate models by providing a short introduction to these models and an application of an illness-death model to the implementation of NPIs in universities in the USA during the Covid-19 pandemic. This example not only demonstrates the ability of multistate models to explore complex processes but also sheds light into the effective implementation of public health interventions.

5.1 Characteristics of Multistate Models

There are three aspects of multistate models that deserve special attention: the state space as defined by number of states in the model, whether the transitions between states are progressive, and the Markov structure of the model. While a full discussion of these characteristics is beyond the scope of this section, the following discussion provides relevant guidelines for the application of multistate models in the social sciences.

5.1.1 State Space

Many survival processes in the social sciences have multiple states. For instance, MPs may be sitting members of parliament for a large period of time – technically since they are first elected as MPs – up to the date when they retire or die in office. Some MPs may be invited to be part of a cabinet, and therefore, they may transition to a state of "cabinet member" for another period of time (although technically they continue to be MPs, this is not relevant in this example). Other MPs may transition from the state of "cabinet member" to the state of "prime minister" at some other point.

In this example, there are three states in the career of an MP: regular MP, cabinet member, and prime minister. In the simplest case, this is a model with *many different* states. In this most simple case, each unit may experience each state only once, which technically eliminates the option of multiple spells. In a more complex and more realistic application, politicians may visit multiple states multiple times. For example, an MP may be a cabinet member with government A only to go back to the benches under government B. Another MP may be a cabinet member with government A and prime minister of government C, only to go back to being a sitting member of parliament and become prime minister of government D, such as Winston Churchill.

In working with multistate models, researchers must specify clearly whether states are transitioning or absorbing and how many states there are in the structure. This will consequently define whether multiple spells are a possibility.

5.1.2 Progressive States

States in multistate models may be progressive, but this is not strictly necessary. For Hougaard (2000: 146), a multistate process is progressive if there is "at most one possible transition into each state, and none into the initial state." In other words, and using Figure 1 as a reference, a model is progressive if there is only one arrow going into each state and none into the initial state, if there is one. If there are multiple paths or arrows into the same state, the model is not progressive.

Progressive models are mathematically convenient. Indeed, some progressive models, such as the competing risks model, are relatively easy to implement, and the quantities of interest are also easy to calculate. Structures that are not progressive are more complex. Consider the ministerial career path mentioned previously. In that case, MPs may transition to the cabinet, with some of them going back to being MPs at some point. Some cabinet members may transition to the prime ministerial state. The same individual may go back to being an MP, like Theresa May, or may opt for retirement. In this light, the model is not progressive because any cabinet member or prime minister may go back to the benches as MP. This will increase the number of relevant transition probabilities, as well as the mathematical complexity.

Models may be transformed from progressive to nonprogressive models, and vice versa, in order to simplify structures or to explore more complex ones. For instance, Metzger and Jones (2016) extend Maeda's competing risks analysis of democratic breakdowns (2010) to a nonprogressive, multistate model where countries can transition back and forth between democracy, exogenously driven autocracy, and endogenously driven autocracy. In another example, a nonprogressive model of political careers of MPs can be transformed into a progressive one whereby MPs may become prime ministers without ever experiencing a period in cabinet. In this case, there are four states: MP, prime minister directly after MP, cabinet member, and prime minster after being a cabinet member. If a prime minister cannot transition from a cabinet position to being a regular MP, this is a fully progressive model. Clearly, this aspect of multistate models is closely related to whether states are transient or absorbing.

5.1.3 Markov Structure

Markov processes lie at the heart of many multistate models. For Hougaard (2000: 142), "the Markov assumption implies that the past and the future are conditionally independent given the present." Many multistate models can be homogeneous or nonhomogeneous Markov processes, or belong to a class of Markov-extension models. Whether the process is homogeneous or nonhomogeneous, or a Markov extension model, depends on the relationship between hazard rates and duration. Hazards that do not depend on time (i.e. constant hazards, such as the hazard in an exponential model) lead to homogeneous processes, while hazards that depend on elapsed-time (i.e. time-dependent hazards) lead to nonhomogeneous processes. The nature of the Markov process in a multistate model has important consequences for the calculation of transition probabilities.

To illustrate the difference between the Markov characteristics of multistate models, consider a set of three states of political institutions: autocracy, mixed regime, and democracy. Assume that the initial state is autocracy and that countries can only transition from autocracy to mixed regime, and from mixed regime to democracy. In this setting, there is no possibility for backsliding. Now consider a hypothetical scenario where a country has been an autocracy from 1980 to 1990 and a mixed regime from 1990 to 1997, when it transitions to democracy.

In a homogeneous process, the transition hazards are constant over time but may vary from state to state. In the previous example, if the hazard rate was constant over time, the probability of transitioning from mixed regime to democracy in the year 1997 depends on the current state of the country (i.e. mixed regime of seven years), but not on the timing of the mixed regime period in total elapsed-time: whether the seven years of mixed regime started in 1990 or in 1986 does not make a difference because the hazard rates are constant over time.

For Beyersmann, Allignol, and Schumacher (2012: 30), the nonhomogeneous Markov property of a process "means that the future course of an individual depends on the past only via the current [elapsed] time and the state currently occupied by the individual." In other words, the probability of transitioning from one state m to another state l depends on total elapsed-time and that the individual is currently on state m, but not on how long the individual has been on state m. Thus, from a nonhomogeneous Markov perspective, the probability of transitioning from mixed regime to democracy depends on the fact that the country is in the "mixed regime" state and that elapsed time is seventeen years, but not on the fact that it has been a mixed regime for seven years.

Additionally, researchers may use Markov-extension models for multistate structures (Hougaard, 2000). In a Markov-extension model, transition probabilities are determined both by elapsed-time to the relevant transition *and* by the timing of the state before the transition takes place. In other words, from a Markov-extension perspective, the probability of transitioning from state m to state l depends on total elapsed time and that the individual is currently on state m and on the timing of the transition into state m. For this reason, Markov-extension models include duration to the state previous to the relevant transition as a covariate in the specification. Note that this is not duration in state m but the time it took the unit to reach state m. Figure 10 presents some of the most important aspects of multistate models.

5.2 From Hazard Rates to Transition Probabilities

Multistate models may have very complex structures with different number of states – some states may be transient or absorbing, or the models may be progressive or behave according to different Markov properties. Regardless of

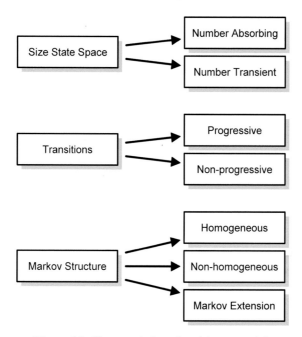

Figure 10 Characteristics of multistate models

the complexity, in a multistate structure, there is a constellation of state-specific transition forces that pull units away from particular states. These transition forces are represented by hazard rates, which vary by state and are often labeled as "cause-specific hazards."

Hazards are informative and have occupied a stellar role in social science applications of survival models. More complex models such as competing risks or multistate models rely on cause-specific hazard rates to calculate cumulative incidence functions or more general transition probabilities. These quantities focus on the probability that units will occupy a particular state at a particular point in time. These quantities are crucial in biostatistics and other fields, and this Element makes a case for their wider use in the social sciences.

Having said this, consider the long-term predictions of the state of a unit, often evaluated at a particular point in time. For instance, we may be interested in the probability that a democratic country will be a mixed regime after 27 years of democracy or after 100 years for that matter. Define X_t as the state occupied by a unit at time $t \geq 0$. Hougaard (2000) defines a transition probability as follows:

$$P_l(t) = Pr(X_t = l). \tag{22}$$

This is the probability that a unit will be in state $X_t = l$ at time t, where t is duration from the initial state or total elapsed-time. Note that this is an unconditional probability suitable for questions such as what is the probability that a democratic country will be autocratic in fifteen years? Or what is the probability that an MP will be prime minister twenty-seven years after they were first elected to parliament?

This transition probability is useful, but it is more useful if it is conditioned on the current state of a unit. For instance, we may be interested in the probability that a country will be democratic in fifteen years given that it is currently a mixed regime or the probability of becoming a prime minister given that an MP is a cabinet minister. We therefore have the following transition probability:

$$P_l(v,t) = Pr(X_t = l | X_u, u \in [0, v]). \tag{23}$$

This is the probability that a unit will be in state $X_t = l$ at time t evaluated at time v where $v \leq t$ (Hougaard, 2000).

The most interesting case is when the unit is in a state m (e.g. mixed regime) at time v where state m is different from state l (e.g. democracy). This defines the following Markov transition probability:

$$P_{ml}(v,t) = Pr(X_t = l | X_v = m), \text{ where } m \neq l \text{ and } v \leq t. \tag{24}$$

This is a very useful transition probability that captures the likelihood that a unit will be in state l at time t given that is in state m at time v.

Going back to our discussion about Markov processes, in a homogeneous process, the probability $P_{ml}(v,t)$ only depends on $t - v$, while in a nonhomogeneous process, the transition probability depends on the interval $[v, t]$ (Hougaard, 2010; Beyersmann, Allignol, & Schumacher, 2012). This is an important difference because nonhomogeneous Markov processes are more general, while homogeneous processes are confined to cases of constant hazard rates.

5.3 Nonparametric Estimates of Multistate Models: Kaplan–Meier, Nelson–Aalen, and Aalen–Johansen Estimators

Semi-parametric estimates of the survivor function and the integrated hazard are crucial in the analysis of multistate models. First, they provide excellent visualizations of a survival process without covariates while avoiding a number of problems caused by the wrong choice of fully parametric distributions. The use of semi-parametric estimates of the survivor function and the integrated hazard relies on a discretization of a continuous survival process (Putter, Fiocco, & Geskus, 2007). As suggested by Hougaard (2000: 69): "The simplest non-parametric estimate of a distribution function is the empirical distribution .... Thus, even though we assume that the true distribution is continuous, we estimate it by a discrete distribution."

Assume that units experience the event of interest at times $t_1, t_2, \ldots, t_k$. Assume that d_j for $j \in [1, k]$ is the number of units that experience the event at time j and that r_j is the number of units at risk of experiencing the event at time $j-$, that is, time just before time j. Then the Kaplan–Meier estimate of the probability of surviving beyond t_j is the the product of the conditional probabilities of surviving through each interval, conditional on having made it to that interval:

$$\hat{S}(t_j) = \prod_{j=1}^{k} \frac{r_j - d_j}{r_j} = \prod_{j=1}^{k} 1 - \frac{d_j}{r_j}. \tag{25}$$

Likewise, the Nelson–Aalen estimator of the cumulative hazard rate is:

$$\hat{\Lambda}(t_j) = \sum_{j=1}^{k} \frac{d_j}{r_j}. \tag{26}$$

The increments d_j/r_j of the Nelson–Aalen estimator are quite interesting because they connect it to the Kaplan–Meier estimate of the survivor function. To see why, recall that the integrated hazard function $\Lambda(t)$ is the area under the hazard rate, which implies that the rate of change at time t of the integrated hazard is the hazard rate: $h(t) = \Lambda(t)'$. In other words, the increments of the Nelson–Aalen estimator of the integrated hazard resemble the hazard rate.

This is important because the Kaplan–Meier estimator of the survivor function can be expressed as a quantity that is a function of the hazard rate. The intuition is as follows. Recall that $\lambda(t) = \lim_{\Delta t \to 0} \frac{Pr(t \leq T \leq t + \Delta t | T \geq t)}{\Delta t}$. In this light, for a unit that has survived up to time t, the instantaneous probability that it will experience the event of interest in the time interval t and $t + \Delta t$ is $\lambda(t)$. Therefore, the probability of surviving beyond time Δt is $1 - \lambda(t)$. This resembles the Kaplan–Meier estimate of the survivor function $1 - d_j/r_j$ at all exit times. In fact, the survival function is an infinite product over conditional probabilities of the type $1 - \lambda(t)$, which leads to its product integral version (Beyersmann, Allignol, & Schumacher, 2012).

The fact that the Kaplan–Meier estimate can be computed as a function of the step changes of the Nelson–Aalen estimator is incredibly important. Indeed, transition probabilities in general can be computed as functions of hazard rates, and their nonparametric estimates can be constructed as functions of step changes in the cumulative hazard, which are reflections of the hazard rate. This is perfectly illustrated by the Aalen–Johansen estimate of the matrix of transition probabilities.

More generally, assume that in a state space of a Markov process, there are two states m and l, where $m \neq l$. For simplicity, assume that it is possible to transition from state m to state l with hazard rate $\lambda_{ml}(t)$. A transition from l to m is also possible, but in this example, it is not necessary. As before, assume that units experience the event of interest at times $t_1, t_2, \ldots, t_k$. Now assume that d_{mlj} is the number of units that experience a transition from m to l at time j where $j \in [1, k]$ and that $d_{mj} = \sum_{m \neq l} d_{mlj}$ is the number of units that exit state m. Define r_{mj} as the number of units at risk of experiencing a transition out of state m. Then the Aalen–Johansen estimator of the matrix of transition probabilities $\boldsymbol{P}(v, t)$ is as follows:

$$\hat{\boldsymbol{P}}(v, t) = \prod_{v < t_j \leq t} (\boldsymbol{I} + \hat{\lambda}_j), \tag{27}$$

where the identity matrix $\boldsymbol{I}$ and the matrix $\hat{\lambda}_j$ have size $(S + 1) \times (S + 1)$, where $S = 0, 1, 2, \ldots, s$ is the number of states in the state space of a Markov process. In this example, there are only two states, m and l, and therefore, $S = 1$. Consequently, the matrices have size 2×2, thus providing cells for all four possible transitions between these two states. Researchers can define which transitions are possible and which ones are not.

In the matrix $\hat{\lambda}_j$, each cell (m, m) is given by $\hat{\lambda}_{mmj} = -\frac{d_{mj}}{r_{mj}}$, and each cell (m, l) is given by $\hat{\lambda}_{mlj} = \frac{d_{mlj}}{r_{mj}}$. For readers interested in calculating these quantities manually, it is important to note that the order of the products is over increasing orders of time; losing this ordering will result in the wrong quantities.

The Aalen–Johansen estimator of the matrix of transition probabilities is crucial for the analysis of multistate models. The estimator is incredibly important in survival analysis in general but so far has been largely ignored in social science applications. On the one hand, the Aalen–Johansen estimator shows that the matrix of transition probabilities $\boldsymbol{P}(v, t)$ can be computed solely as a function of hazard rates. This simplifies calculations and highlights the importance of hazard rates as the building block of multistate models. On the other hand, and for particular models, the Aalen–Johansen estimator nests a number of other probabilities, such as the survivor function in the mortality model, or the cumulative incidence function for competing risks models. Altogether, the Aalen–Johansen estimator addresses a number of challenges in the estimation of survival models in a compact and intuitive calculation.

5.3.1 Application: Transitions from Democracy to Autocracy

To illustrate the importance of the Aalen–Johansen estimator, consider the following example of democratic countries that may transition to autocracy.

Table 9 An example of survival data

Time Interval (Months)	Number of Units at Risk of a Transition	Number of Units with a Transition
(0–1]	5	1
(1–2]	4	2
(2–3]	2	1

This is a mortality model with two states: democracy (d) and autocracy (a). Democracy is the initial state, and autocracy is an absorbing state; this is not a realistic assumption, but it is a useful one in this example. We are interested in two transition probabilities: $P_{dd}(v, t)$ and $P_{da}(v, t)$. The former is the probability that a democracy at time v will be a democracy at time t, for $v < t$. The latter is the probability that a democracy at time v will be an autocracy at time t. In other words, $P_{dd}(v, t)$ is the probability of surviving as a democracy, and $P_{da}(v, t)$ is the probability of a transition to autocracy. As mentioned, autocracy is assumed to be absorbing, and therefore, a country that has transitioned to autocracy will remain an autocracy. Even in this case, we must define two additional transition probabilities: $P_{aa}(v, t)$ and $P_{ad}(v, t)$. The former is the probability that an autocracy will survive as an autocracy, which is simply one because autocracy is an absorbing state. The latter is the probability that an autocracy will transition to a democracy, which is zero also because autocracy is an absorbing state.

In sum, the matrix of transition probabilities $P(v, t)$ has two rows and two columns as follows:

$$P(v, t) = \begin{bmatrix} P_{dd} & P_{da} \\ P_{ad} & P_{aa} \end{bmatrix}. \tag{28}$$

In order to estimate these probabilities, we need data. Thus, consider the following artificial data in Table 9 for the duration of democracy in five countries.

In this example, all five countries are democratic at time zero; this is the initial state. By the end of the first month of democracy, one country has transitioned to autocracy. At the beginning of the second interval, the number of countries at risk of experiencing a transition is four because one country already transitioned to autocracy. By the end of the second month of democracy, two more countries transitioned to autocracy. At this point, a total of three countries have become autocratic. Therefore, at the beginning of the third interval, the number of countries at risk of experiencing a transition is two. By the end of the third month of democracy, another country has transitioned to autocracy. By month three, only one democracy survives.

The goal in this example is to estimate transition probabilities from the origin at time zero to a duration of three months. We can estimate these transition probabilities using the Aalen–Johansen estimator. First, there are two states, democracy and autocracy, and therefore, $S = 1$. Second, for the entire time interval (0–3], there are transitions at (0–1], (1–2], and (2–3]. Therefore, the transition probabilities in the interval (0–3) will have three components, each with $j = 1, 2, 3$. Note that j denotes the duration in months at the end of the interval.

Also, recall that d_{mlj} is the number of units that experience a transition from m to l at time j and that $d_{mj} = \sum_{m \neq l} d_{mlj}$ is the number of units that exit state m. In this specific example of autocratic transitions, $d_{daj} = d_{dj}$ because there are only two states, "d" and "a," and because units can only transition from "d" to "a." In other words, the only destination out of state "d" is "a," and therefore, all units exiting state "d" go to "a."

Having said this, for the interval (0–1], we have the following:

$$(I + \hat{\lambda}_1) = \begin{bmatrix} 1 & 0 \\ 0 & 1 \end{bmatrix} + \begin{bmatrix} -1/5 & 1/5 \\ 0 & 0 \end{bmatrix} = \begin{bmatrix} 4/5 & 1/5 \\ 0 & 1 \end{bmatrix}.$$

For the interval (1–2], we have the following:

$$(I + \hat{\lambda}_2) = \begin{bmatrix} 1 & 0 \\ 0 & 1 \end{bmatrix} + \begin{bmatrix} -2/4 & 2/4 \\ 0 & 0 \end{bmatrix} = \begin{bmatrix} 1/2 & 1/2 \\ 0 & 1 \end{bmatrix}.$$

For the interval (2–3], we have the following:

$$(I + \hat{\lambda}_3) = \begin{bmatrix} 1 & 0 \\ 0 & 1 \end{bmatrix} + \begin{bmatrix} -1/2 & 1/2 \\ 0 & 0 \end{bmatrix} = \begin{bmatrix} 1/2 & 1/2 \\ 0 & 1 \end{bmatrix}.$$

We can then multiply these matrices to obtain $\hat{P}(v,t) = \prod_{v < t_j < t}(I + \hat{\lambda}_j)$.

$$\hat{P}(0,3) = \begin{bmatrix} 4/5 & 1/5 \\ 0 & 1 \end{bmatrix} \begin{bmatrix} 1/2 & 1/2 \\ 0 & 1 \end{bmatrix} \begin{bmatrix} 1/2 & 1/2 \\ 0 & 1 \end{bmatrix} = \begin{bmatrix} 1/5 & 4/5 \\ 0 & 1 \end{bmatrix}.$$

Going back to our original question for estimating the matrix of transition probabilities, the Aalen–Johansen estimate is:

$$\hat{P}(0,3) = \begin{bmatrix} P_{dd} & P_{da} \\ P_{ad} & P_{aa} \end{bmatrix} = \begin{bmatrix} 1/5 & 4/5 \\ 0 & 1 \end{bmatrix}.$$

In words, the probability of surviving as a democracy P_{dd} beyond year 3 is 1/5, and the probability of transitioning to autocracy P_{da} by year 3 is 4/5. Since autocracy is an absorbing state, $P_{ad} = 0$ and $P_{aa} = 1$.

Of course, in the mortality model, it is not necessary to perform these calculations. Rather than calculating the Aalen–Johansen estimate, we could simply calculate the Kaplan–Meier estimate of the survivor function for the interval $(0,3]$. The Kaplan–Meier estimate of the probability of surviving beyond month three is:

$$\hat{S}(3) = \prod_{j=1}^{3} 1 - \frac{d_j}{r_j} = \frac{(4)(1)(1)}{(5)(2)(2)} = \frac{1}{5}.$$

With the estimated CDF equal to $\hat{F}(3) = 1 - \hat{S}(3) = 4/5$. Here, $\hat{S}(3)$ and $\hat{F}(3)$ are exactly the two quantities in the top row of the Aalen–Johansen estimate $\hat{P}(0,3)$. This is because in the mortality model, the Aalen–Johansen estimate produces the Kaplan–Meier estimate and its complement. The interested reader can check that computing the Aalen–Johansen estimate for all time intervals reproduces all the values of the Kaplan–Meier estimate.

It is important to note that this equivalency only applies to the mortality model. Once the Aalen–Johansen estimate is applied to more complex multistate models, this equivalency is lost, and instead, the Aalen–Johansen estimate produces transition probabilities, including cumulative incidence functions. This difference was highlighted in the previous discussion about competing risks. Indeed, the Aalen–Johansen estimate is quite flexible because the term d_{mj} considers all exits from the state m regardless of destination, while the term d_{mlj} considers exits to the particular destination l. In the context of competing risks, this is equivalent to using $S(t)$ and not the naïve $S_k(t)$. In other words, the Aalen–Johansen produces estimates of cumulative incidence function. It just happens that the cumulative incidence function is equivalent to the CDF in the mortality model because there is only one destination.

5.4 An Illness-Death Multistate Model: NPIs in University Campuses during Covid-19

The section now uses data on the NPIs implemented by US universities during the height of the Covid-19 pandemic in order to introduce more complex multistate models and transition probabilities.

During outbreaks of contagious diseases, including Covid-19, universities often implement NPIs. During the pandemic, these included social distancing, working remotely, and closing campuses, among others (Quiroz Flores et al., 2021). The timing for the implementation of NPIs can be modeled as competing risks – a university that has not implemented any protection measures must choose carefully the type and timing of NPIs, as each intervention comes with great cost to students, staff, the university, and the community that surrounds it.

In implementing NPIs, time is of the essence. For instance, a university may choose to encourage social distancing or move to online teaching or implement remote working or even close a campus. Facing a pandemic, universities made one choice or another, but eventually most universities implemented most of these measures in a sequence during the pandemic (Cevasco et al., 2020). By the end of 2020, schools and universities in over 150 countries had closed their doors, interrupting the education of 1.5 billion learners.

The sequence of university NPIs provides an excellent opportunity to illustrate multistate models. The section uses original data on 575 US universities collected in March 2020 (Cevasco et al., 2020). The data focuses on five NPIs (Cevasco et al., 2020): (1) moving classes online, (2) encourage students to leave on-campus accommodation, (3) cancel university-sponsored travel, (4) close campus, and (5) remote work for staff and faculty. The section focuses on two interventions: (1) remote work and (2) closing a campus. Cevasco et al.'s data (2020) provides the dates for these two interventions across universities, which are used in this section to create duration variables. Specifically, the variables count the number of days from December 31, 2019, to the date for remote work and the date for closing a campus for each university. This date in December is the date when the WHO first identified a statement from Wuhan Municipal Health Commission related to a new viral pneumonia. The median duration for "Remote work" is 76 days, with a mean of 76.2 days and a variance of 16.3 days. The median duration for "Close campus" is 79 days, with a mean of 80.4 days and a variance of 26.04 days.

The data suggests that a majority of universities closed their campus shortly after implementing remote working, although there is considerable variance in the timing of interventions. Thus, the goal of the analysis is to explore the effect of covariates on these transitions. While there is a large body of work on the implementation of university NPIs, the analysis of the timing of these interventions remains understudied. Quiroz Flores et al. (2021) use a series of indicators to explore the timing of Covid-19-related communication in UK universities, including university size, financial resources, and prevalence of Covid-19 cases in the vicinity of a campus. This section relies on a simpler specification that focuses on the natural logarithm of the cumulative number of Covid-19 positive cases in the state where the university is located at the time when the university implemented remote working (*ln(Covid Cases)*), the natural logarithm of the number of full time students in a university (*ln(Students)*), and the party of the state governor (*Governor Party*).

The section focuses on three states. In state 1, the initial state, universities have not implemented any NPIs. In state 2, universities have implemented remote working. In state 3, universities have closed their campus. During the

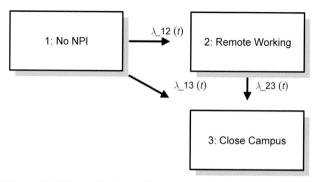

Figure 11 Illness-death multistate model without recovery of nonpharmaceutical interventions in US universities

pandemic, universities technically could move from one state to another, but universities seldom did this (Cevasco et al., 2020). Instead, they either transitioned from state 1 to state 2 to state 3 or transitioned from state 1 immediately to state 3. Most universities first implemented a policy of remote work and then closed their campuses, but some universities closed their campuses without implementing a policy of remote work. When universities implemented a policy of remote work and closed a campus on the same day, this is counted as a transition to closing a campus. Note that state 2 can only be reached via state 1, which assumes that universities cannot go back to remote work after closing a campus. In other words, state 3 is an absorbing state, while state 2 is a transitioning state, and state 1 is the initial state. It is also assumed that universities cannot transition back from remote work to the initial state. Altogether, this is known as an illness-death model without recovery. This structure is presented in Figure 11.

5.4.1 Transition Probabilities

In this example, there are three transitions, each with its own transition force or hazard rate. The first type of transition is from state 1 to state 2, with cause-specific hazard rate $\lambda_{12}(t)$. The second type of transition is from state 2 to state 3, with hazard $\lambda_{23}(t)$. The third type of transition is from state 1 to state 3, with hazard $\lambda_{13}(t)$. Two transition forces pull a university out of state 1, that is $\lambda_{12}(t)$ and $\lambda_{13}(t)$, and therefore, the all cause hazard rate from state 1 is $\lambda_{1.}(t) = \lambda_{12}(t) + \lambda_{13}(t)$.

Multistate models focus on long-term transition probabilities. Define $P_{11}(v, t)$ as the probability that a university in state 1 at time v will remain in state 1 at time t. In other words, this is the probability of "surviving" in state 1 or, equivalently, that there is no transition to state 2 or 3. To calculate this probability, recall that $S(t) = \exp(-\Lambda(t)) = \exp(-\int_0^t \lambda(u)du)$. Based on this logic, the multistate model considers the two destinations out of state 1 and their transition forces that pull a unit out of state 1, that is, $\lambda_{12}(t)$ and $\lambda_{13}(t)$. Consequently, the transition probability $P_{11}(v,t)$ is:

$$P_{11}(v,t) = \exp(-\int_v^t \lambda_{12}(u) + \lambda_{13}(u)du). \tag{29}$$

Since state 1 is assumed to be an initial state, it is possible to set $v = 0$, but it is useful to denote it in the more general case v.

The second probability $P_{12}(v,t)$ is the probability that a university in state 1 at time v will be in state 2 at time t. This is the probability that a university that has not implemented an NPI at time v will be implementing remote working at time t. In other words, it is the probability of being in state 2 evaluated at a particular time during state 1. Analytically, this probability has two components: (1) the likelihood of leaving state 1 and reaching state 2 and (2) the likelihood of remaining in state 2 after the transition from state 1.

The first component of $P_{12}(v,t)$ is the probability of leaving state 1 for state 2; note that this is not the transition hazard but the probability of failure (toward state 2) before time t. In other words, this is a cumulative incidence function similar to the function presented in the section of competing risks. This incidence function will have the components $P_{11}(v,t)$ and $\lambda_{12}(t)$, which represent the survivor function in state 1 and the transition force toward state 2.

The second component of $P_{12}(v,t)$ is the survivor function in state 2, that is, the probability of remaining in state 2 after making the transition from state 1. Indeed, a university in state 2 can transition to state 3 with positive probability, and therefore, in calculating the probability that a university in state 1 at time v will be in state 2 at time t, we must account for the likelihood of surviving in state 2. Define $P_{22}(u,t)$ as the probability of surviving in state 2 after transitioning from state 1, where $v \leq u \leq t$. Here, the calculation of $P_{22}(.)$ is similar to the computation of $P_{11}(v,t)$: once in state 2, a university can only transition to state 3, and therefore, we need to compute the probability that this transition will not take place. Taking into consideration that there is only one transition force $\lambda_{23}(t)$ out of state 2, then $P_{22}(u,t) = \exp(-\int_u^t \lambda_{23}(s)ds)$. In terms of the complement of this probability, since there is only one exit out of State 2, this is $P_{23}(u,t) = 1 - P_{22}(u,t)$.

We now have all the elements of $P_{12}(v,t)$, which is defined as follows (Borgan, 1997):

$$P_{12}(v,t) = \int_v^t P_{11}(v,u)\lambda_{12}(u)P_{22}(u,t)du. \tag{30}$$

This is a fascinating probability that accounts for the survivor probability in state 1 (i.e. $P_{11}(v,u)$), the transition force toward state 2 (i.e. $\lambda_{12}(t)$), which together would form the cumulative incidence function in state 1. It also accounts for the probability of surviving in state 2 after the transition via $P_{22}(u,t)$. Hougaard (2000) gives an excellent interpretation of these terms for a progressive version of the illness-death model. His intuition is as follows (Hougaard, 2000: 158): "first, the unit survives in state 1 from time v to time u, which is captured by $P_{11}(v,u)$. Then there is a transition at time u, captured by $\lambda_{12}(u)$. Then the unit stays in state 2, which is captured by $P_{22}(u,t)$."

The final quantity in this illness-death model is the probability that a university in state 1 at time v will remain in state 3 at time t, which is denoted by $P_{13}(v,t)$. In the example, this is the likelihood that a university that has not implemented a NPI at time v will be closing its campus at time t. Note that state 3 is absorbing, and therefore, there are no transitions back from this state. In this light, we can compute $P_{13}(v,t) = 1 - (P_{11}(v,t) + P_{12}(v,t))$. For a different calculation of $P_{13}(v,t)$, readers may consult Beyersmann, Allignol, and Schumacher (2012).

The probabilities of interest, $P_{11}(v,t)$, $P_{12}(v,t)$, and $P_{13}(v,t)$, without covariates, can be estimated using the Aalen–Johansen estimator of the matrix of transition probabilities $\boldsymbol{P}(v,t) = \prod_{v < t_j \leq t}(\boldsymbol{I} + \hat{\lambda}_j)$. In this case, there are three states, and therefore, $S = 2$. The matrix of transition probabilities $\boldsymbol{P}(v,t)$ has three rows and three columns as follows:

$$\boldsymbol{P}(v,t) = \begin{bmatrix} P_{11} & P_{12} & P_{13} \\ P_{21} & P_{22} & P_{23} \\ P_{31} & P_{32} & P_{33} \end{bmatrix}. \tag{31}$$

The logic for the computation of quantities across cells is identical to the mortality model. The complexity arises from two modifications. First, starting from the initial state when universities have not implemented any NPIs, there are competing risks: state 2 (remote work) and state 3 (close campus). Second, state 2 is a transitioning state, and units can transition from state 2 to state 3. However, the complexity ends there, as the model has two simplifying assumptions. First, units are not allowed to transition from state 2 back to state 1, and therefore, conditional on reaching state 2, this is a nested mortality model for transitions to state 3. Second, state 3 is absorbing. Of course, these are not realistic assumptions, as universities eventually moved back to face-to-face teaching, but they are useful for the purposes of demonstrating multistate models.

The nonparametric estimation of these transition probabilities entails accurate and detailed counting of cases to calculate $\hat{\lambda}_{mmj} = -\frac{d_{mj}}{r_{mj}}$ for each cell (m,m)

and $\hat{\lambda}_{mlj} = \frac{d_{mlj}}{r_{mj}}$ for each cell (m, l). For example, for the three states 1, 2, and 3 over the interval (v, t), we have the following:

$$(I + \hat{\lambda}_j) = \begin{bmatrix} 1 & 0 & 0 \\ 0 & 1 & 0 \\ 0 & 0 & 1 \end{bmatrix} + \begin{bmatrix} -\frac{d_{1j}}{r_{1j}} & \frac{d_{12j}}{r_{1j}} & \frac{d_{13j}}{r_{1j}} \\ \frac{d_{21j}}{r_{2j}} & -\frac{d_{2j}}{r_{2j}} & \frac{d_{23j}}{r_{2j}} \\ \frac{d_{31j}}{r_{3j}} & \frac{d_{32j}}{r_{3j}} & -\frac{d_{3j}}{r_{3j}} \end{bmatrix}.$$

However, because units are not allowed to transition from state 2 back to state 1 and because state 3 is absorbing, this yields:

$$(I + \hat{\lambda}_j) = \begin{bmatrix} 1 & 0 & 0 \\ 0 & 1 & 0 \\ 0 & 0 & 1 \end{bmatrix} + \begin{bmatrix} -\frac{d_{1j}}{r_{1j}} & \frac{d_{12j}}{r_{1j}} & \frac{d_{13j}}{r_{1j}} \\ 0 & -\frac{d_{2j}}{r_{2j}} & \frac{d_{23j}}{r_{2j}} \\ 0 & 0 & 0 \end{bmatrix}.$$

The Aalen–Johansen estimator, like the Kaplan–Meier, may be calculated over periods of time. Figure 12 presents the Aalen–Johansen nonparametric estimates of four key transition probabilities: the probability not implementing any NPI (i.e. P_{11}), the probability of a transition from lack of interventions to remote work (i.e. P_{12}), the probability of a transition from a state of remote work to closing a campus (i.e. P_{23}), and the probability of a transition from lack of interventions to remote work (i.e. P_{13}).

These empirical estimates are quite informative. The most noticeable aspect of these graphs is the large change in probabilities around day eighty, which is close to March 20, 2020. At this time, during the initial stage of the pandemic, the probability of transitioning from the status quo, marked by the absence of major interventions, to remote working (i.e. P_{12}) is highest. Many universities that had transitioned to a state of remote working also made a transition to closing their campus (i.e. P_{23}) around March 20. Notice that P_{23} resembles a cumulative distribution function because $P_{23} = 1 - P_{22}$, where P_{22} is the survivor function in state 2. Here, the term CDF – as opposed to cumulative incidence function – is adequate because, as mentioned before, conditional on reaching state 2, this is a nested mortality model for transitions to state 3. Indeed, all universities in state 2 eventually transitioned to state 3, closing a campus. The same trend emerges for the transition from a state of absence of NPI to campus closure (i.e. P_{13}): those universities that did not implement a policy of remote working, eventually transitioned to closing their campus, with the largest number of transitions also taking place around March 20, 2020. This is consistent with the findings of Cevasco et al. (2020), which indicate that the largest number of transitions to remote working took place around March 16–17, with a steep increase in the number of university closures between March 16 and 20.

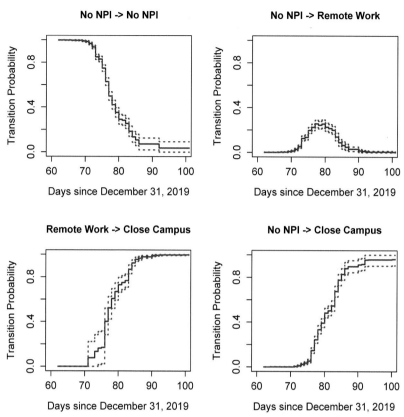

Figure 12 Transition probabilities for the illness-death multistate model of nonpharmaceutical interventions in US universities. Estimates from the empirical Aalen–Johansen estimator. Ninety-five percent confidence interval in dashed pink lines. Estimates were produced by the following *R* code: etm<-etm(pone_long_na,c("1","2","3"),tra,"cens", s=0), where tra is a transition matrix, "cens" is a censoring indicator, and s=0 is a starting value for probabilities

5.4.2 Estimation

Semi-parametric estimation via Cox proportional hazard models can be used to calculate the effect of covariates in multistate models. The estimation of these models is relatively straightforward. The challenge resides in organizing the data in a format that is suitable for the packages that estimate multistate models and produce the relevant quantities of interest. The package *mstate* in *R* provides excellent tools to transform typical social science data sets to *mstate* format.

As an example, consider the cross-section of 575 US universities discussed previously. The database records the date when each university implemented a

Table 10 Data point for a university

Remote Work: Yes/No	Days to Remote Work	Close Campus: Yes/No	Days to Close Campus
1	72	1	82

particular NPI. The database also contains information about the characteristics of each university. The first step in preparing data for the analysis of multistate models is the set up of the transition matrix. The transition matrix determines how many states there are in a model and which transitions are allowed to take place. Indeed, the transition matrix defines how many states there are in a structure and whether these states are transitioning or absorbing. This can be done using 0/1 indicators across the cells of a matrix or by numbering the available transitions.

In the case of universities, we have three states: absence of NPIs, remote work, and closing a campus. Therefore, the transition matrix will be a 3 × 3 matrix. As mentioned before, the data as it is does not allow transitions from state 2 (remote work) to state 1 (no NPI). Likewise, state 3 is absorbing, and therefore, there are no transitions from state 3 (close campus) to state 2 or 1. Further research may relax these assumptions about potential transitions. Having said this, the transition matrix for the case of universities is as follows:

$$\text{tmat} = \begin{bmatrix} NA & 1 & 2 \\ NA & NA & 3 \\ NA & NA & NA \end{bmatrix}$$

Additional steps that select covariates of interest are described in the replication files. However, it is relevant to describe the data output produced by the *msprep* call in the package *mstate*. Consider the data in Table 10 for a university in the data set.

It is assumed that all universities start at the same state, that is, state 1: no NPI. This university experienced a transition from the initial state, no NPI, to remote work, indicated by the value of 1 in column 1. If it had not experienced that transition, the value for that column would be 0. It took 72 days from December 31, 2019, to implement this intervention. The university also experienced a transition from state 2 (remote work) to state 3 (close campus), which is indicated in column 3. This transition took place on day 82 from December 31, 2019.

The *msprep* call transforms the previous observation into three different observations in a count format that is similar to the setup of survival data with

Table 11 Extended data for a university

From	To	Transition	Tstart	Tstop	Time	Status
1	2	1	0	72	72	1
1	3	2	0	72	72	0
2	3	3	72	82	10	1

multiple records. The key variables in the extended data set for the university described previously are presented in Table 11.

The first row indicates the origin state (state 1) and the destination state (state 2), as well as the transition number (1) defined in the transition matrix. Row 1 also indicates the origin time (0 days) and the time of the event of interest (72 days), that is, a transition to remote work. The row also indicates the duration in the state (72 days) and whether the event actually took place (1), as recorded by the column Status. The second row indicates that this university did not transition from state 1 to state 3, as shown by the 0 in the column Status. The third row indicates a transition from the origin state (state 2) to another state (state 3) and records the transition number (3). It also records the origin time from state 2 (72 days) and the time of the event of interest (82 days), that is, close campus. The duration in state 2 is 10 days. The occurrence of the transition to state 3 indicated by the number 1 in the column Status.

It is important to note that not all observations for each university are extended into three observations. Only the universities that experienced all three states will have three observations in the extended data set. Universities that only experienced two states will have two observations in the extended data set. All universities in the data set experienced at least two states: the initial states marked by the absence of NPIs and either remote work or closure of a campus.

Additions to the *msprep* call will also set transition-specific covariates. The multistate models presented next control for the natural logarithm of the number of students in a university, among other variables. Using this example, the transition-specific values for this variable are presented in Table 12. These transition-specific covariates are implemented for practical reasons in the estimation of the multistate model.

To review, the first step in the estimation of a multistate model is the definition of the transition matrix. This can be done manually or by using available transition matrices in the package *mstate*. The second step requires a careful transformation of the data into a format that can be used for estimation. This

Table 12 Transition-specific covariates in extended data for a university

Transition	Ln(Students).1	Ln(Students).2	Ln(Students).3
1	10.7	0	0
2	0	10.7	0
3	0	0	10.7

Table 13 Illness-death multistate model of NPIs in US universities. Unit: US university. Standard errors in parentheses. Estimation results produced by the following *R* code: mstate1<-coxph(Surv(Tstart,Tstop,status) ~ Zs + strata(trans), data=ponelong, ties="efron"). Note that the censoring indicator status is a factor

Variable	Coefficient
Ln(Covid Cases).Tr1	−0.4 (0.0)
Ln(Covid Cases).Tr2	−0.3 (0.1)
Ln(Covid Cases).Tr3	0.1 (0.0)
Ln(Students).Tr1	0.4 (0.1)
Ln(Students).Tr2	0.0 (0.1)
Ln(Students).Tr3	0.1 (0.1)
Governor Party.Tr1	−0.4 (0.1)
Governor Party.Tr2	−0.3 (0.1)
Governor Party.Tr3	−0.1 (0.1)
Observations	1,293
Failures	810

can be done with the *msprep* call in the package *mstate*. The third step complements the *msprep* call in order to carefully set transition-specific covariates. It is strongly recommended that researchers check the quality of the transformed data to make sure that it accurately represents the transitions observed in the sample. It is worth noting that at the time of writing, time-varying covariates are not available for estimation for multistate models and that data used for estimation is originally set up as single-record data.

Having transformed the data into the correct format, estimation is as simple as the estimation of any Cox model in *R* using the package *survival*. Table 13 presents results from a Cox proportional hazard model applied to a multistate structure as defined before. The model does not make assumptions about proportional covariates and instead uses stratification, as determined by the transition number, in order to estimate separate baseline hazards (Putter, Fiocco, & Geskus, 2007).

The estimation results of a multistate model can be approached from two perspectives. First, researchers may focus on the analysis of hazard rates based on coefficients. As mentioned before, hazard rates are key quantities on their own, and they provide important information about the forces that pull units out of their current state. In this case, the previous results reflect the effects of coefficients on each transition as defined by the transition matrix and illustrated in Figure 11. As an example, the coefficient for the natural logarithm of the number of students is 0.4, which is statistically significant at the 95 percent level. This indicates that student population increases the hazard rate for the transition from state 1 to state 2, that is, from no NPI to remote work. Interestingly, the coefficients for *Governor Party* are either negative or not statistically significant, which indicates that the hazard rate of implementing any NPI decreases if the state governor is Republican.

The second strategy for interpretation focuses on transition probabilities. As mentioned, the Markov assumption in multistate models allow for the estimation of the probability that a unit in some state m at time v will be in state l at time t, often for $v < t$. These are probabilities that may help stakeholders answer key questions related to the timing of interventions, and that is why these quantities are so crucial in biostatistics. In our example of universities, a student may want to know what is the probability that a university that has not implemented any intervention by late February 2020 will close its campus in late March. This would allow the student to make plans for leaving campus accommodation. Note that this is a different approach relative to hazard rates, which concentrates on the forces that lead universities to transition from state to state. Indeed, rather than knowing whether a covariate increases or decreases the hazard rate of a particular transition, the focus is on estimating the probabilities that units will be in different states. This is the essence of transition probabilities.

In order to produce transition probabilities, it is first necessary to calculate baseline cumulative hazards. Cumulative hazards are important because they show the rate of change in the hazard rate, thus proving an indication of the velocity in the accumulation of risk over time. In addition, they are the bridge between hazard rates and other key quantities of interest, such as survivor functions and other transition probabilities. Figure 13 presents the baseline cumulative hazards for different transitions after estimation.

These are quite striking cumulative hazards. On the one hand, the cumulative hazards for the transition from no NPI to remote work (i.e. $\hat{\Lambda}_{12}$) and from remote work to close campus (i.e. $\hat{\Lambda}_{23}$) are quite flat, indicating a slow

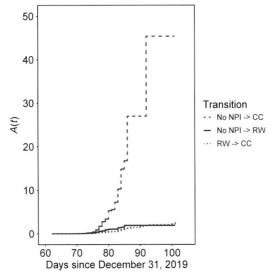

Figure 13 Estimated baseline cumulative hazards. Based on estimation results from the illness-death multistate model of Table 13. Estimates were produced by the following *R* code: `msf1.0<-msfit(mstate1, newdata=nyu0, trans=tmat)`, where `newdata` uses the number of transitions while setting other covariates to zero and `tmat` is a transition matrix. Full *R* code is available at https://doi.org/10.7910/DVN/ADZUEA

and even decreasing rate of accumulation of risk. In contrast, the cumulative hazard for the transition from no NPI to close campus (i.e. $\hat{\Lambda}_{13}$) shows a very fast accumulation of risk, mostly in between days 77 and 85, which is around March 20, 2020. This is consistent with situations where universities that did not implement protective measures before March 20 were forced to accelerate the closure of their campus ahead of lockdowns.

Having calculated and presented cumulative hazards, researchers may focus on transition probabilities, which are complex quantities that combine information from hazard rates, cumulative hazards, and survivor functions in a nonlinear form. Empirical transition probabilities were calculated at the beginning of the section using the empirical Aalen–Johansen estimator. These quantities can also be calculated after estimating a Cox model.

It is strongly recommended that researchers choose carefully the presentation of results, as these calculations require information about the origin state of the unit (e.g. no NPI) and the transition to another state (e.g. close campus), as well as specific points in time for the prediction. The careful selection of starting points is particularly crucial because it determines the starting point of the time axis. Figure 14 presents transition probabilities from state 1, no NPI, from a starting point of 0 days.

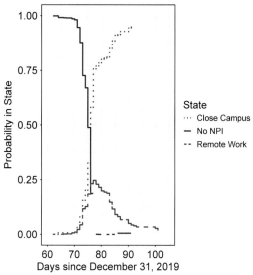

Figure 14 Estimated baseline transition probabilities from state 1: no NPI. Aalen–Johansen estimates based on results from the illness-death multistate model of Table 13 and the estimated baseline cumulative hazards in Figure 13. Estimates were produced by the following *R* code:
```
aj0<-probtrans(msf1.0, predt=0, direction="forward",
method="greenwood"),
```
where predt=0 is the starting time for the prediction and direction="forward" is the direction of the prediction

These quantities closely resemble the results from the empirical Aalen–Johansen estimator. The purple line is essentially a survivor function and indicates the probability of transition from state 1 (no NPI) to state 1 (no NPI). In other words, this is an estimate of the lack of a transition from state 1, which, clearly, decreases over time, as universities were forced to take action to mitigate the effects of the pandemic and protect students and staff through the implementation of interventions. The probability of transitioning from state 1 (no NPI) to state 2 (remote work) shows a jump close to day 80 and then a steep drop, as it was also demonstrated in Figure 12 with the empirical Aalen–Johansen estimator. The probability of transition from state 1 (no NPI) to state 3 (close campus) increases over time, with a dramatic increase just after day 70, around March 10.

5.5 Summary

Multistate models have been available in biostatistics for at least twenty years. These models play a key role in the analysis of clinical pathways whereby patients experience different states of health or illness over multiple times. In this setting, the prediction of transition probabilities are central for treatment, as clinicians need to have an understanding of the future state of patients.

This type of complex multistate structure is less prevalent in empirical applications in social sciences. Theoretically, typical units of analysis in social sciences such as countries, states, or politicians, may visit multiple states over the course of a "lifetime," such as a political career or a relationship with a neighbouring country. Unfortunately, data collection for these units does not always follow up on multiple transitions; this is a costly and complex enterprise that limits the amount of data collected in social sciences. Nevertheless, as data collection improves, it is recommended that multistate structures are considered as a framework for analysis. Collecting information about multiple spells, multiple states and their characteristics, as well as the covariates for relevant units, should consider a multistate format.

Computational methods for analyzing this type of data are now available. In this context, it is highly recommended that researchers implement quality control of any data prepared for the analysis of multistate models. In addition, researchers should have a good understanding of probability in order to take full advantage of these models. As a first step in the analysis, researchers may focus on the analysis of hazard rates, but they should be aware of the multiple rates present in these structures and the associated challenges that come with this approach.

Having done this, researchers can proceed with the analysis of transition probabilities to answer questions related to future states of relevant units of analysis. It is highly recommended that researchers are confident with the selection of parameters used in the interpretation of estimation results. As long as the data are correctly set up for a multistate structure, estimation via Cox proportional hazards models is relatively simple. However, the calculation of predictions after estimation is quite sensitive, and researchers should consider the options that are best suited to answer their research questions.

5.6 Further Readings

The Element highly recommends Hougaard's *Analysis of Multivariate Survival Data* (2000), which presents a detailed overview of multistate models, including all the necessary probability concepts and calculations of very complex transition probabilities for many multistate structures, from nonhomogeneous Markov models to Markov transition models, and progressive and nonprogressive structures, among many others. Interested readers should also study Borgan (1997), as it presents an excellent analysis of the Aalen–Johansen estimator of the matrix of transition probabilities, as well as other relevant empirical estimates such as the Nelson–Aalen estimator of the cumulative hazard.

The package *mstate* provides tools to process and transform data into a format that facilitates the estimation of multistate models. The package also provides techniques for estimation and interpretation of results. Putter, Fiocco, and Geskus (2007) presents a detailed coverage of multistate models and competing risks. This section relies heavily on Putter's "Tutorial in biostatistics: competing risks and multistate models. Analyses using the *mstate* package" (2021), which is a very thorough tutorial on multistate models. Putter, Fiocco, and Geskus (2007) present alternative formats for the estimation of an illness-death model. Putter's tutorial can be complemented by Beyersmann, Allignol, and Schumacher (2012), who present a series of alternative calls in *R* to model multistate processes. Therneau, Crowson, and Atkinson (2021) also provide a useful overview of these models. All of these works will offer similar visualizations of the menu of models covered in this Element, including those in Figure 1. In social sciences, Metzger and Jones (2016) present an excellent discussion and application of multistate models to political science.

6 Conclusion

Survival analysis consists of a set of models suitable for the study of time to an event. The hazard rate is at the center of these models and social scientists often estimate the effects of covariates on this quantity using a Cox proportional hazards model. The Cox model assumes that covariates have a proportional effect on the hazard rate over time; breaking this assumption obliterates the raison d'être of the Cox model. For this reason, the Element offers new guidelines in hazard analysis, including proper model specification to avoid a false positive of nonproportionality and the correct use of timescales in tests of nonproportional covariates. Researchers should follow these guidelines carefully in order to accurately asses a potential failure of the proportionality assumption. If there is evidence of nonproportional covariates, researchers should implement a correction and use the new methods covered in this Element to correctly interpret the effect of covariates on the hazard rate.

The Element makes a case for the use of alternative quantities of interest in survival analysis, such as cumulative incidence functions and more general transition probabilities. The computation of these quantities relies on hazard rates, which confirms the key role of hazard analysis in empirical work. Transition probabilities help researchers answer questions that address the long-term probabilities that units will occupy a state as some time t given that they occupy a different state at some other time v. This type of approach is particularly important in policy analysis because it informs the design and implementation of interventions that reduce the likelihood that units will fall into unwanted states. In this light, this Element presents transition probabilities as key quantities of interest in competing risks and more general multistate survival models.

Multistate survival models are the most general form of survival models and provide a structure for the analysis of very complex survival processes. These models have been available in biostatistics for decades, but researchers have only just begun to apply them to substantive questions in the social sciences. This Element encourages researchers to consider and study multistate models as a general framework for survival analysis. However, in order to make the most of this approach, it is important that researchers gain a strong command of probability theory. This is beneficial on its own but will also equip researchers with powerful tools to model and understand survival processes.

References

Beyersmann, Jan, Arthur Allignol, and Martin Schumacher. 2012. *Competing Risks and Multistate Models with R (Use R!)*. New York: Springer.

Boehmke, Frederick J. 2009. "Policy emulation or policy convergence? Potential ambiguities in the dyadic event history approach to state policy emulation." *Journal of Politics* 71(3): 1125–40.

Borgan, Ørnulf. 1997. *Three Contributions to the Encyclopedia of Biostatistics: The Nelson-Aalen, Kaplan-Meier, and Aalen-Johansen Estimators*. Preprint series. Statistical Research Report.

Box-Steffensmeier, Janet M., and Bradford S. Jones. 2004. *Event History Modelling: A Guide for Social Scientists*. Cambridge: Cambridge University Press.

Box-Steffensmeier, Janet M., Suzanna De Boef, and Kyle A. Joyce. 2007. "Event dependence and heterogeneity in duration models: The conditional frailty model." *Political Analysis* 15: 237–56.

Carter, David B., and Curtis S. Signorino. 2010. "Back to the future: modeling time dependence in binary data." *Political Analysis* 18(3): 271–92.

Cevasco, Kevin E., Hayley M. North, Sheryne A. Zeitoun et al. 2020. "COVID-19 observations and accompanying dataset of non-pharmaceutical interventions across U.S. universities, March 2020." *PLoS ONE* 15(10): e0240786.

Cox, David R. 1972. "Regression models and life-tables." *Journal of the Royal Statistical Society B* 34(2): 187–220.

Fine, Jason P., and Robert J. Gray. 1999. "A proportional hazards model for the subdistribution of a competing risk." *Journal of the American Statistical Association* 94(446): 496–509.

Gandrud, Christopher. 2015. "simPH: An R package for illustrating estimates from cox proportional hazard models including for interactive and nonlinear effects." *Journal of Statistical Software* 65(3): 1–20.

Goemans, Henk E., Kristian Skrede Gleditsch, and Giacomo Chiozza. 2009. "Introducing Archigos: A data set of political leaders." *Journal of Peace Research* 46(2): 269–83.

Grambsch, Patricia M., and Terry M. Therneau. 1994. "Proportional hazards tests and diagnostics based on weighted residuals." *Biometrika* 81(3): 515–26.

Haller, Bernhard, Georg Schmidt, and Kurt Ulm. 2013. "Applying competing risks regression models: An overview." *Lifetime Data Analysis* 19(1): 33–58.

Hougaard, Philip. 2000. *Analysis of Multivariate Survival Data*. New York: Springer.

Jin, Shuai, and Frederick J. Boehmke. 2017. "Proper specification of nonproportional hazards corrections in duration models." *Political Analysis* 25: 138–44.

Jones, Benjamin T., and Shawna Metzger. 2019. "Different words, same song: Advice for substantively interpreting duration models." *PS: Political Science & Politics* 52(4): 691–95.

Keele, Luke. 2010. "Proportionally difficult: Testing for nonproportional hazards in Cox models." *Political Analysis* 18(2): 189–205.

Licht, Amanda A. 2011. "Change comes with time: Substantive interpretation of nonproportional hazards in event history analysis." *Political Analysis* 19(2): 227–43.

Maeda, Ko. 2010. "Two modes of democratic breakdown: A competing risks analysis of democratic durability." *Journal of Politics* 72(4): 1129–43.

Metzger, Shawna K., and Benjamin T. Jones. 2016. "Surviving phases: Introducing multistate survival models." *Political Analysis* 24(4): 457–77.

Metzger, Shawna K., and Benjamin T. Jones. 2021. "Properly calculating estat phtest in the presence of stratified hazards." *The Stata Journal* 21(4): 1028–33.

Park, Sunhee, and David J. Hendry. 2015. "Reassessing Schoenfeld residual tests of proportional hazards in political science event history analyses." *American Journal of Political Science* 59(4): 1072–87.

Przeworski, Adam, Michael E. Alvarez, Jose Antonio Cheibub, and Fernando Limongi. 2000. *Democracy and Development: Political Institutions and Well-Being in the World, 1950–1990.* Cambridge: Cambridge University Press.

Putter, Hein. 2021. *Tutorial in Biostatistics: Competing Risks and Multi-state Models. Analyses Using the mstata Package.* Comprehensive R Archive Network (CRAN). https://cran.r-project.org/web/packages/mstate/vignettes/Tutorial.pdf

Putter, Hein, Marta Fiocco, and Ronald B. Geskus. 2007. "Tutorial in biostatistics: Competing risks and multi-state models." *Statistics in Medicine* 26(11): 2389–430.

Quiroz Flores, Alejandro, Farhana Liza, Husam Quteineh, and Barbara Czarnecka 2021. "Variation in the timing of Covid-19 communication across universities in the UK." *PLoS ONE* 16(2): e0246391.

Schemper, Michael. 1992. "Cox analysis of survival data with non-proportional hazard functions." *Journal of the Royal Statistical Society: Series D* 41(4): 455–65.

Therneau, Terry M. 2020. *Package "coxme": Mixed Effects Cox Models*. Comprehensive R Archive Network (CRAN). https://cran.r-project.org/web/packages/coxme/index.html

Therneau, Terry M., Cynthia Crowson, and Elizabeth Atkinson. 2021. *Multi-state Models and Competing Risks*. Comprehensive R Archive Network (CRAN). https://cran.r-project.org/web/packages/survival/vignettes/compete.pdf

Therneau, Terry M., and Patricia M. Grambsch. 2000. *Modeling Survival Data: Extending the Cox Model*. New York: Springer.

Therneau, Terry M., Thomas Lumley, Atkinson Elizabeth, and Crowson Cynthia. 2022. Package "survival": Survival Analysis. Comprehensive R Archive Network (CRAN). https://cran.r-project.org/web/packages/survival/index.html

Acknowledgments

I would like to thank the series editors, Neal Beck and R. Mike Alvarez, as well as Cambridge University Press, for the opportunity to publish this Element. It has given me the chance to organize and present material that I have accumulated over more than ten years of teaching survival analysis. I am particularly grateful to Neal for the discussions, suggestions, and all the feedback he has given me as I prepared and wrote the Element.

I also want to thank Christoph Dworschak and Katharina Pfaff for invaluable feedback and great suggestions. Two anonymous reviewers also gave very useful feedback that improved the manuscript. Nicola Rowley provided excellent proofreading. I also thank many students and teaching assistants at Essex, Waseda, and NYU, who have taken my survival analysis courses and given many useful comments on how to present this material for learning purposes.

I would also like to acknowledge the support of the Business and Local Government Data Research Centre (ES/S007156/1) funded by the Economic and Social Research Council (ESRC) for undertaking this work.

Lastly, I want to thank my wife, Barbara, for many conversations on how to teach statistics and for her support while I wrote this Element. The Element is dedicated to my son, Alex, who loves science.

Cambridge Elements ≡

Quantitative and Computational Methods for the Social Sciences

R. Michael Alvarez

California Institute of Technology

R. Michael Alvarez has taught at the California Institute of Technology his entire career, focusing on elections, voting behavior, election technology, and research methodologies. He has written or edited a number of books (recently, *Computational Social Science: Discovery and Prediction*, and *Evaluating Elections: A Handbook of Methods and Standards*) and numerous academic articles and reports.

Nathaniel Beck

New York University

Nathaniel Beck is Professor of Politics at NYU (and Affiliated Faculty at the NYU Center for Data Science) where he has been since 2003, before which he was Professor of Political Science at the University of California, San Diego. He is the founding editor of the quarterly, *Political Analysis*. He is a fellow of both the American Academy of Arts and Sciences and the Society for Political Methodology.

About the Series

The Elements Series Quantitative and Computational Methods for the Social Sciences contains short introductions and hands-on tutorials to innovative methodologies. These are often so new that they have no textbook treatment or no detailed treatment on how the method is used in practice. Among emerging areas of interest for social scientists, the series presents machine learning methods, the use of new technologies for the collection of data, and new techniques for assessing causality with experimental and quasi-experimental data.

Cambridge Elements ☰

Quantitative and Computational Methods for the Social Sciences

Elements in the Series

A Practical Introduction to Regression Discontinuity Designs: Foundations
Matias D. Cattaneo, Nicolás Idrobo and Rocío Titiunik

Agent-Based Models of Social Life: Fundamentals
Michael Laver

Agent-Based Models of Polarization and Ethnocentrism
Michael Laver

Images as Data for Social Science Research: An Introduction to Convolutional Neural Nets for Image Classification
Nora Webb Williams, Andreu Casas, and John D. Wilkerson

Target Estimation and Adjustment Weighting for Survey Nonresponse and Sampling Bias
Devin Caughey, Adam J. Berinsky, Sara Chatfield, Erin Hartman, Eric Schickler, and Jasjeet S. Sekhon

Text Analysis in Python for Social Scientists: Discovery and Exploration
Dirk Hovy

Unsupervised Machine Learning for Clustering in Political and Social Research
Philip D. Waggoner

Using Shiny to Teach Econometric Models
Shawna K. Metzger

Modern Dimension Reduction
Philip D. Waggoner

Text Analysis in Python for Social Scientists: Prediction and Classification
Dirk Hovy

Interpreting Discrete Choice Models
Garrett Glasgow

Survival Analysis: A New Guide for Social Scientists
Alejandro Quiroz Flores

A full series listing is available at: www.cambridge.org/QCMSS

Printed in the United States
by Baker & Taylor Publisher Services